FABULOUS RECIPES FROM ASIA'S FOOD CAPITAL

SINGAPORE
Cooking

Terry Tan & Christopher Tan

Foreword by David Thompson
Photography by Edmond Ho

TUTTLE Publishing

Tokyo | Rutland, Vermont | Singapore

T0019829

Contents

Foreword

A Deep-Seated Passion For Food

Call me biased, but I think the best reason for visiting Singapore is the food. If Singaporeans aren't eating a meal, then they are either talking about it or planning for the next. This passion does not stem merely from some culinary hedonism—although pleasure surely plays a large part—but from some deep-seated belief that the sharing of food and its preparation binds a family and community together. Even more so when the food tastes so good.

Perhaps the true strength of Singaporean food lies in its diverse background and the willingness of the people to embrace new tastes and ingredients. Chinese, Malay, Indian and Nonya cuisines are both maintained and blended into one of the world's most interesting, delicious cuisines. Whatever the reason the result is food that tastes … shiok!

The Jackfruit Curry and Gulai Prawns make me want to go to the market and then into the kitchen. The Fishhead Curry could easily do a winning lap on Race Course Road. The Satay or Hainanese Chicken Rice are happily reminiscent of that served in the old Beach Road or Middle Road restaurants. In this book, culinary favourites such as these are presented in an enticing style with truly alluring photographs.

I have known both Terry and Christopher Tan for several years and have always been impressed with their conviction and knowledge. This wonderful book is the outcome.

David Thompson

Shiok!

Some wag once said that the quickest way to start a debate in Singapore is to walk up to a random group of people and ask them, "So where can I get the best chicken rice?"

Eating is the Singapore national sport. An irresistible vein of foodieness runs deep in the Singaporean genetic makeup. We plan lunch over breakfast and dinner over lunch, and then go out to supper. We incessantly trade tips about the best places to get the shiokest dishes. Our Chinese wedding dinners stretch to nine courses over four hours. We endure forty minutes of queueing for a simple bowl of ground pork noodles with black vinegar. Why? Because we can't find the particular flavour of the stall's old-fashioned chilli sauce anywhere else.

There is a such diversity of ways and places to stuff your face here, from hawker centres and corner coffeeshops to the classiest contemporary Asian and Western restaurants. You can empty your wallet for a French dinner one night and sit down to a $1 *dosai* (south Indian rice crêpe) the next morning. Given the details of our island republic's history, our egalitarian omnivorousness is no surprise. Over the centuries before and since its founding in 1819 by the Englishman Sir Stamford Raffles, Singapore has had a cultural life braided with Chinese, Malay, Arab, Thai, Indian, Indonesian, Eurasian, colonial British and continental influences. Our cuisine, then and now, reflects this. How else to explain a Chinese chicken soup with macaroni, crispy shallots and fried bread croutons? A rich curry of pork ribs and bamboo shoots? A Hainanese chef's special "chicken cutlets" in HP Sauce-spiked brown gravy with chips and peas? A staple breakfast trio of hot buttered toast slathered with coconut-egg jam, a soft-boiled egg drizzled with dark soy sauce and a cup of thick, black, highly sweetened coffee? When you grow up with such an eclectic mix of edibles, your taste buds get a uniquely intoxicating education.

Top left to right: Beautifully mottled crab shells; man serving up chicken curry at the Adam Road food centre; Middle left to right: A well-connected roast meat stall at the Tiong Bahru food centre; deep-fried "butterfly" buns; fish seller at the Chinatown Complex market; Bottom left to right: Durian, the king of fruits; used condensed milk cans make handy takeaway coffee cups; otak-otak or barbecued fish in banana leaves.

Chinese Cooking: Dialectical Differences

Forget the greasy homogeneity of the oriental takeaway menu too often found abroad. The true diversity of Chinese cuisine is as wide and deep as regional French or Italian. There is no "Chinese food" *per se*—there is food from Hunan and Swatow and Beijing and Yunnan and Shanghai and that's without considering the web of Chinese ancestry extending throughout South-East Asia, the Thai-Teochews, Indonesian Chinese and so on, each strand of which has its own culinary distinctions.

Terry comes from the match of an Indonesian Chinese father and a mother whose antecedents came from the early Peranakan clans of Malacca, Penang and Thailand. Then again, his father's family also had Hokkien roots in China's Fujian Province and his mother's family a branch of good Teochew stock from the Swatow district of Guangdong Province. Every family feast was a glorious *tok panjang*—the Peranakan festive offering of dishes spread across a long table. Chris' maternal grandfather was a true-blue Baba who married a true-blue Cantonese lady and their house-hold meals were an eclectic mix of classics from both worlds, brought together in a mouth-watering alchemy.

In essence, Chinese food in Singapore has four main regional branches—Hokkien, Teochew Cantonese and Hainanese. Teochews are inordinately fond of soups, braised dishes and steamed dishes, clear and relatively unadorned. Hokkiens stir up delicious noodle dishes and meat rolls. And the Cantonese are masters at roasted meats and simply sauced vegetables and seafood. The most celebrated contribution of the Hainanese, apart from the scores of *ah kors* or male chefs who manned the woks and ovens of country club kitchens and Western restaurants—some of whom still do today—is the aforementioned chicken rice, which by now has evolved into something quite different from the original dish cooked on Hainan Island.

These *précis* do not of course do full justice to the full range of regional Chinese cuisines, which is displayed as much in home kitchens as in restaurants. Other Chinese styles of cooking, such as Shanghai, Hunan, Sichuan and such only noticeably established themselves as part of the local landscape from the mid-1950s onwards, as Chinese from those parts migrated here. Much in evidence these days too are the contemporary strains of Chinese cooking informed by Hong Kong-style Cantonese cuisine, French techniques and the occasional South-East Asian flavour, which have a great sense of adventure and vibrancy to them.

Malay Flavours: Rasa Sayang

Malay cooking has a revered—though not always loudly acknowledged—place within the Singapore kitchen as a major evolutionary influence, in the same way Indian and Indonesian cuisines do. The fresh spices and herbs of the Malaysian Peninsula and the dry, aromatic ones of Arabic Muslim and Indian Muslim origins combine in the intricate weave of local Malay food. Who has eaten *nasi lemak* and not remembered its delicate nuances? Some of Terry's fondest childhood memories are of our neighbourhood Malay hawkers who sold little banana leaf packets of this coconut rice, topped with Crispy Ikan Bilis with Peanuts, a fried egg and a rich, hot Fried Chilli Sambal to dab on it all. And there are still few satays to beat those made by Malay chefs, Terry's favourite being *satay babat*, made with tripe. The rich coconut, palm sugar and rice flour in Indonesian and peninsular Malay desserts has also left its mark on Nonya sweets.

Indian Influences: Spice-laden Breezes

Historically, most of Singapore's Indian inhabitants came from the south of the sub-continent—Tamils and Malayalees mainly. Later came the Sindis, Gujaratis, Bengalis and Punjabis from the northern provinces and presently the square kilometer that makes up

Little India is redolent with their combined gastronomical talents. It is a disservice to summarise India's cuisines in anything less than several hundred pages, but as a rough reference for the palate, southern Indian food in Singapore is characterised by rice flour-based breads as well as rice dishes, with an abundance of seafood, fresh vegetables, cool yoghurt and sour tamarind as foils for aromatic, chilli-hot spice blends spiked with mustard seeds and curry leaves. Northern Indian food here calls more often on wheat breads as the staple and boasts many rich and complex curries as well as tandoori specialties. A meal of either ilk is typically built around a mix of dry and wet dishes and chutneys and pickles. One "Indian" curry, made with large fish heads in a spicy, sour gravy, is in fact a uniquely Singaporean variation on a Keralan theme that you won't find in the motherland.

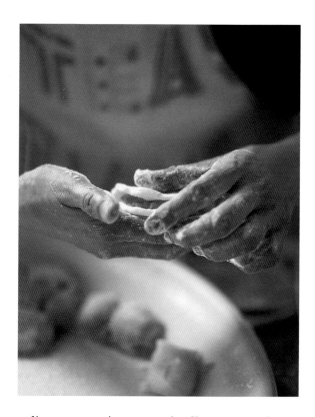

Peranakan Roots: Our Own Fusion Heritage

Also known as Straits Chinese, the Peranakan people (the latter term meaning "born of the soil") have roots in Chinese, Malay and Indian culture. The respectful term for Peranakan men, Baba, comes from an Indian word; women are called Nonyas. The original community arose centuries ago in Malacca and today the other centres of the diaspora are in Penang and Singapore, with small groups in Indonesia and Thailand. Each community has its own distinct culinary emphases. Malaccan and Singaporean Nonya food is largely similar, but many Nonya dishes from Penang, further north, have a Thai mood about them and the Penangite patois embraces many Thai words. Many Peranakans were of Chinese-Indonesian parentage, like my father; the nearby Riau Islands were a Peranakan outpost.

All told, it makes for scrumptious eating—a natural example of "fusion" cuisine—without any of the hapless connotations that word has gathered in the modern era. The Peranakan culinary canon integrates its diverse roots into a glorious whole. It includes curries of seafood, beef and chicken, but also pork; braised meats almost purely Chinese in style, but enlivened with a snap of spices; fattening festive noodle dishes and healthy salads of raw vegetables and herbs; and rich desserts that will have you napping after lunch. Perhaps its most iconic dish is chicken and pork ribs cooked in a spicy tamarind gravy with *buah keluak*, Indonesian black nuts whose meat tastes divinely like the offspring of a black truffle, a dark chocolate bar and wet earth after rain.

The best Nonya cooks, like cooks everywhere, measure ingredients and cooking times with their hands, eyes, noses and ears, and they give a name to this cooking by feel—*agak-agak*. Much of Terry's own style in this respect was handed down to him by first his grandmother and then his mother, bless their Nonya souls, who in assigning him sometimes tedious kitchen tasks made him an unwitting trustee of the culture. Chris was not forcibly steeped in his ancestry in the same way, but picked it up through osmosis, as it were.

As food writers, our sense of our heritage reminds us that we have a duty to arouse curiosity and passion about food culture in future generations, to instill a respect for tradition as well as a level-headed appreciation for innovation. We must all learn to care about our food traditions enough to prevent them from slipping away, to keep the precious legacy of our parents' and grandparents' kitchens alive and bright. We hope that this book will spur you on to do that.

How To Use This Book

This book was written for three kinds of people. One is the Singaporean who doesn't cook much, but wants to get to know his own food heritage better. The second is the intrepid non-Singaporean who wants to broaden his culinary horizons. Welcome to our world! The third is everyone else. Why would anyone want to miss out on some great food?

If your desire to stir up something delicious is tempered by a vague idea of cooking as a complex, tedious process and therefore a dreaded chore, be reassured that none of these recipes are particularly difficult. A few require a dedicated investment of time and all benefit from your full attention—the unexamined dish is not worth eating, after all—but, trust us, the returns are worth it.

Cooking once was more labourious, true. Buying a chicken also used to mean killing, de-feathering, blood-letting and butchering it. Terry has severed his fair share of chickens' jugulars, scoured neighbourhood hedges for the *bunga telang* flowers his mother would press a dark blue-purple dye from to colour her *ang koo kueh* (mung bean and rice flour cakes) and taken countless bus rides to the seashore to gather, at low tide, tons of wet, slimy, icky seaweed to be dried in the sun, boiled down, clarified, and cooked with sugar and water to make the delicious agar-agar jelly for Chinese New Year desserts.

But that was long ago. Nowadays, you don't have to coax damp wood to make a fire in a *hung lo* (earthenware) oven—a museum piece nowadays—or grind your own rice flour, or even peel your own shallots (though it does build character). Shopping for and cooking local food can be a source of pure pleasure. We urge you to take the time to explore your local wet market. Smell the herbs, pat the vegetables, watch the butchers and fishmongers carve up their charges and above all chit-chat with the stallholders and their regular customers, who are invariably founts of culinary information. You will learn, if you haven't already, how to choose fruit and vegetables, how to appraise seafood with a wise eye, what this spice and that gourd is for, how to best portion a chicken for a family of five. This is knowledge not on sale at the supermarket, which though convenient and clean—and fast, if you're pressed for time—lacks the sheer exuberance of the open-air Asian pasar.

Chris, a former psychology student, likes to think of cooking as therapy; the sequence of shopping, assembling, prepping and following the final sequence of steps is a contemplative, creative and deeply satisfying activity. Taking a recipe and experimenting with it until it has gotten under your skin requires no less art and gives no less joy than learning to play a Chopin étude. We urge you to *agak-agak*, to judge and adjust quantities of ingredients on the fly, to imbue the dishes with your own personal touch.

This collection of recipes is a personal and idiosyncratic one. It is not meant to be a definitive guide to Singaporean gastronomy—as if such a thing could be contained in a single volume!—nor is it an anonymous collation of ersatz ethnic expressions packaged for painless digestion. These dishes are drawn from our lives, from the home repertoires we have cooked our way through many times over the years. They are what we enjoy eating. We hope you find them shiok too!

Singapore Ingredients

Assam gelugor is the Malay name for the sweet-sour garcinia fruit that resembles a dried apple. Dried slices of the fruit are used as a fruity souring agent in place of tamarind pulp in some Malay and Nonya dishes.

Thai basil
(horapa)

Lemon basil
(mangkak)

Asian basil (*daun kemangi*) is used as a seasoning and garnish, and there are several varieties. The most common is known as **Thai basil** or *horapa* and is fairly similar to European and American sweet basil. It is used liberally as a seasoning and sprigs of it are often added to platters of fresh raw vegetables. **Lemon basil** or *manglak* is similar to *horapa* but paler and with a distinctive lemony fragrance. It is used in soups and salads. Asian basils are commonly available in Asian food stores and many supermarkets, and Italian basil makes an acceptable substitute.

Asian eggplants in Singapore are generally of the slender, purple-skinned variety, 15–20 cm (6–8 in) long. They are mild and need not be salted before use.

Asian shallots are small and round and have a pinkish-purple colour. Shallots add a sweet oniony flavour and a hint of garlic to countless dishes. They are also sliced, deep-fried and used as a garnish.

Bamboo shoots are the fresh shoots of the bamboo plant and make an excellent vegetable. Fresh shoots taste better than canned, but must be peeled, sliced and simmered in water for about 30 minutes before using. Ready-to-use sliced bamboo shoots, packed in water, can be found in the refrigerated produce section of some supermarkets and are convenient and easy to use. Canned bamboo shoots should be blanched for 5 minutes to refresh them before using. Both fresh and canned bamboo shoots are increasingly available in many supermarkets.

Banana leaves infuse a delicate flavour and aroma to food. They are often used as wrappers when steaming or grilling dishes, or as little trays to hold food when cooking. Soften the leaves slightly in boiling water for about 10 seconds before use to prevent them from cracking and tearing when wrapping foods.

Bangkuang is a root vegetable native to tropical America, where it is known as jicama. It has a crunchy white flesh and beige skin that peels off quite easily. It is excellent eaten raw, sliced and served with rock salt or dressing as a refreshing snack. Substitute daikon radish.

Basmati rice is an Indian long-grain rice characterised by its fragrance. The grains stay whole and separate when cooked with oil and spices. Substitute Thai jasmine rice.

Bean sprouts are sprouted from mung beans. Soybean sprouts are available but are less common. Purchase sprouts fresh as they lose their crisp texture quickly. They will keep for a few days if stored in the refrigerator immersed in a tub of water.

Black Chinese mushrooms, also known as shiitake mushrooms, are large and meaty, and are used in many recipes throughout this book. Fresh shiitake are increasingly available in supermarkets although porcini mushrooms, or **dried black Chinese mushrooms** may be used as well. If using dried mushrooms, soak in hot water for 10 to 15 minutes to soften, then drain and discard the stems before dicing or slicing the caps. **Wood ear mushrooms** are also called wood ear fungus, and are tree mushrooms that have a crunchy texture and a delicate woodsy flavour. They are available both fresh and dried in Chinese markets and are dark brown to black in colour. Soak dried mushrooms in hot water until soft. Substitute shiitake or porcini mushrooms. **Straw mushrooms** are grown on rice straw found in paddy fields, hence their name. They are small, light brown mushrooms with tiny caps, thin stems and a musty, earthy flavour. These mushrooms are a popular addition to Asian soups and stir-fries. Available in Asian markets either fresh, canned or dried.

Wood ear
mushrooms

Black Chinese
Mushrooms

Belimbing is a pale green, acidic fruit about 5–7 cm (2–3 in) long, often added to curries, soups and pickles. It belongs to the same family as the starfruit and is sometimes called baby starfruit.

Black moss fungus (*fatt choi*) is a fine, hair-like fungus valued in Chinese cooking. Soak in warm water before using.

Chillies are indispensable in Asian cooking. The commonly-used fresh green and red Asian **finger-length chillies** are moderately hot. Tiny red, green or yellow-orange chilli padi or **bird's-eye chillies** are very hot, designed for strong palates. **Dried chillies** are usually cut into lengths and soaked in warm water to soften before use. Dried chillies have a very different flavour from fresh ones. To reduce the heat, discard some or all of the chilli seeds before preparation as part of a spice mix. **Ground red pepper,** also known as cayenne, is a hot seasoning made from ground dried chillies. It is not the same as Mexican ground red pepper which contains a mix of paprika, cumin, thyme and other spices. Western paprika is also relatively milder and tastes completely different from Asian ground red pepper. **Chilli oil** is made from dried chillies or ground red pepper infused in oil, which is used to

Dried chillies

Fresh finger-length chillies

Bird's-eye chillies

enliven some Sichuan dishes. **Chilli sauce** is made by mixing ground chillies with water and seasoning the mixture with salt, sugar and vinegar or lime juice. It is available bottled and in jars.

Bok choy is a highly nutritious type of cabbage with long, crisp stalks and spinach-like leaves. It has a clean, slightly peppery flavour and is a wonderful addition to soups and stir-fries. Baby bok choy is the small, tender variety of bok choy. Bok choy is available in most well-stocked supermarkets.

Bunga telang (butterfly pea) flowers, picked fresh from their vine or dried, yield a vivid indigo blue juice when crushed in water, that is used for colouring various kueh (cakes).

Candlenuts are waxy, cream-coloured nuts similar in size and texture to macadamia nuts, which can be used as a substitute, although less expensive raw almonds or cashews will also do. Candlenuts are never eaten raw or on their own, but are chopped, ground and cooked with seasonings and added to curries and spice mixes for their oil and texture. They go rancid quickly because of their high oil content, so buy them in small quantities and keep them refrigerated.

Cardamom pods are used to flavour curries and desserts—giving foods a heady, sweet scent. The fibrous, straw-coloured pods enclose 15–20 pungent, black seeds. Whole pods are bruised lightly with a cleaver or a pestle before use. Try not to use ground cardamom as it is virtually flavourless compared to the whole pods.

Chinese cabbage, also known as Napa cabbage, has white stems that end in tightly packed pale green leaves. It has a mild, delicate taste.

Chinese celery is often referred to in Singapore as "local" celery. The stems are very slender and more fragrant than normal celery—more of a herb than a vegetable. The leaves are generously used to garnish a variety of Chinese dishes. Substitute celery leaves or Italian parsley.

Chinese chives, or garlic chives, have flattened leaves and resemble thin green onions (scallions). They have a strong garlicky flavour and are often added to noodle or stir-fried vegetable dishes during the final stages of cooking. Substitute green onions, although their flavour is more mild.

Choy sum is a leafy green vegetable with slightly crunchy stems. Available in supermarkets in Asia, choy sum is now increasingly available in Western countries too. Substitute any other crisp leafy greens.

Cockles (hum) are tiny shellfish that are also known as blood cockles or blood clams. They are usually very briefly blanched or fried before being eaten. Cockles are known to carry hepatitis, so be careful where you buy them and cook them thoroughly.

Coriander leaves, also known as cilantro or Chinese parsley, are used as a herb and garnish. Fresh coriander leaves should keep for 5 to 6 days if you wash and dry the leaves thoroughly before placing them in a plastic bag. Dried **coriander seeds** (*ketumbar*) are round and beige, and are perhaps the most widely used spice in India. When ground they release a warm, nutty, slightly citrus-like aroma. Whole coriander seeds have a stronger flavour than ground dried coriander powder, which quickly loses its aroma.

Coconut milk or **cream** are used in many dishes in Singapore in much the same way that milk or cream are used in Western cooking. They are made by squeezing the flesh of freshly grated mature coconuts. To obtain **coconut cream**, about ½ cup (125 ml) water is added for each grated coconut, then squeezed and strained. **Thick coconut milk** is obtained by adding 1 cup (250 ml) of water to the grated coconut, then pressing it to extract the juice. **Thin coconut milk** is obtained by adding another 2 cups (500 ml) of water to the already squeezed grated coconut and pressing it a second time. Although freshly pressed cream and milk have more flavour, they are now widely sold canned and in packets which are quick, convenient and quite tasty. Canned or packet coconut cream or milk comes in varying consistencies depending on the brand, and you will need to try them out and adjust the thickness by adding water as needed. In general, you should add 1 cup (250 ml) water

to 1 cup (250 ml) canned or packet coconut cream to obtain thick coconut milk, and 2 cups (500 ml) water to 1 cup (250 ml) coconut cream to obtain thin coconut milk. These mixing ratios are only general guides and you should adjust the consistency to individual taste. **Desiccated coconut** is **grated coconut flesh** that has been finely ground and dried. Sweetened and unsweetened **coconut flakes** of several sizes are sold in packets, usually in the baking section of supermarkets.

Cumin seeds are pale brown to black in colour and ridged on the outside. They impart an earthy flavour and are used whole, or roasted and ground to a fine powder. Cumin seeds are usually partnered with coriander seeds in basic spice mixes, and are often dry-roasted or fried in oil to intensify their flavour.

Curry leaves are an important herb in southern Indian cooking. The small, dark green leaf has a distinctive flavour which is sadly missing from the dried herb. When a sprig of curry leaves is called for in a recipe, this means 8–12 individual leaves.

Daikon radishes are large root vegetables also known as "white carrots" or "turnips" in Singapore. They are juicy but bland, unlike the smaller western radish. They can grow to a length of 40 cm (15 in) or more. Choose firm and heavy daikons without any bruises. Scrub or peel the skin before you grate or slice the flesh.

Dried prawns are a popular ingredient in sauces and sambals. They are tiny, orange-coloured sun-dried saltwater prawns. They keep for several months and should be soaked in water for 5 minutes to soften slightly before use. Dried prawns come in various sizes and the very small ones have the heads and tails attached. Look for dried prawns that are pink and plump. Better quality dried prawns are bright orange in colour and shelled.

Dried prawn paste is a dense mixture of fermented ground prawns with a very strong odour that may be offensive to some. Also known by its Malay name, *belachan*, it is sold in blocks that range in colour from caramel to dark brown. Small pieces should be sliced from the brick and roasted before use—either wrapped in foil and dry-roasted in a wok or skillet, or toasted over an open flame on the end of a fork or back of a spoon—to enhance the flavour and kill bacteria. In some recipes, dried prawn paste is ground with the rest of the ingredients and fried in oil without toasting. It is not to be confused with fermented prawn sauce (*hay koh*) which tastes and smells different.

Dried sweet Chinese sausages (*lap cheong*) are sweet, reddish sausages delicately perfumed with rice wine. They are used as an ingredient in stir-fries or braised dishes rather than being eaten on their own like European sausages. Sold in pairs, they keep almost indefinitely without refrigeration.

Fennel is similar in appearance to cumin although slightly longer and fatter. Fennel has a sweet fragrance that is similar to aniseed. Some Indian cooks wrongly translate *saunf*, the word for fennel, as aniseed, but the latter spice is not found in India. The seeds are used whole or ground.

Fermented beancurd comes in two varieties—white fermented (*foo yee*) and red fermented (*lam yee*). Both are used as a condiment or seasoning.

Fenugreek seeds are flat and slightly rectangular, about 3 mm (⅛ in) across, light brown in colour, with a deep furrow along their lengths. They are used in Indian cuisines and are quite bitter, so use sparingly.

Fish sauce is the ubiquitous condiment used in almost every Thai or Vietnamese dish, just as salt or soy sauce are used in other cuisines. Made from salted, fermented fish or prawns, it has a very pungent, salty flavour in its pure form. Fish sauce is often combined with other ingredients such as sugar, garlic and lime juice to make the various dipping sauces. Use sparingly and always look for a quality brand for a better flavour. Refrigerate after opening.

Five spice powder is a blend of five ground dried spices—cinnamon, cloves, fennel, Sichuan pepper and ginger. It is sold in small packets in the spice section in most supermarkets.

Galangal is a fragrant root similar to ginger. It imparts a distinctive fragrance and flavour to many South-East Asian dishes. Try to find young, pinkish galangal as they are more tender. Always peel and slice the root before grinding as it is tough. Galangal is available dried, frozen and packed in water, but try to get the fresh root whenever possible as it is far more fragrant.

Garam masala is a blend of several strongly aromatic spices such as coriander, cumin, pepper and cardamom, designed to add flavour and fragrance to meat dishes. Pre-blended garam masala can be bought from any store specializing in spices. Store the ground powder in an airtight jar away from heat or sunlight.

Ginkgo nuts have a hard shell and are spherical in shape. The Korean variety is small, green and tender on the inside, unlike the common Chinese variety. Shelled white nuts are sold in Asian food stores in two forms—either refrigerated in plastic packets or canned. If using whole unshelled ginkgo nuts, boil them in water for about 7 minutes, drain and crack open to remove the hard shells. Soak the nuts in water to loosen the skins around them.

Glutinous rice flour is made from white glutinous rice grains that are ground into a powder. It is stickier than normal rice flour and is generally used in dumplings, buns and pastries. You can buy it in packets in most Asian food stores.

Hay koh (fermented prawn sauce) is a black, pungent, molasses-like seasoning made of fermented prawns, salt, sugar and thickeners. It is sold in jars and cans, and is used as a sauce or a dip. It is sometimes labelled as *petis* and is unrelated to *belachan*.

Hoisin sauce is made from fermented soybeans, garlic, chillies, sugar and vinegar. The sauce is thick and dark and has as sweet, salty flavour. Commercially bottled or canned hoisin sauce is available in most grocery stores.

Ikan bilis or dried baby anchovies are tiny whitebait fish ranging from 2–5 cm (1–2 in) in length. They are usually sold in Asia salted and sun-dried. Remove the head and black intestinal tract before using. If possible, buy them already split, cleaned and ready for use. *Ikan bilis* are usually quite salty, so taste any dish using *ikan bilis* before adding more salt. They are used as a seasoning or deep-fried with chillies and peanuts to make a crunchy side dish or appetiser (see recipe on page 27).

Jackfruit, or *nangka*, is a large, green fruit with a tough, knobbly skin, which reveals bright yellow segments when opened. The yellow flesh has a taste that is naturally sweet and fragrant. Readily available fresh in South-East Asia, the fruit can be purchased canned in the West.

Kai lan, also known as Chinese broccoli or Chinese kale, has long, narrow stems and leaves, and small edible flowers. The stems are the tastiest part while the leaves are slightly bitter. Chinese broccoli is available fresh in Asian markets. Substitute broccoli stems, bok choy or broccolini.

Kaffir lime leaves (*daun limau purut*) add an intense fragrance to Malay and Nonya soups and curries. The leaves are added whole to curries, or finely shredded and added to salads, giving them a wonderfully tangy flavour. Kaffir lime leaves are sold fresh in the herb section of Asian markets and are available frozen or dried in Asian specialty stores in the West. Frozen leaves are more flavourful than dried ones.

Kangkong, or water spinach, is a nutritious, leafy vegetable also known as morning glory or water convolvulus. The leaves and tender tips are often stir-fried. Bok choy or spinach make good substitutes.

Laksa leaves, also called *daun kesom*, polygonum or Vietnamese mint, are traditionally added to spicy laksa soup dishes. The spear-shaped leaves wilt quickly once they are plucked from the stem. They have an intense fragrance reminiscent of lemon with a hint of eucalyptus. There is no real substitute, but a mixture of spearmint and coriander leaves or basil does approximate its flavour and fragrance.

Lemongrass is a fragrant, lemony stalk that is either bruised and used whole in soups or curries, or sliced and ground as part of a basic spice mix. It is usually sold in bunches of 3–4 stems in the supermarket. The tough outer layers should be peeled away and only the thick lower third of the stem used. Always slice the stems before grinding to get a smooth paste.

Longans grow in clusters. The fruit has a brown skin and sweet, crunchy, juicy flesh. Also available in cans. Chinese dry goods stores sell whole dried unshelled longans, and also shelled, stoned raisin-sized nuggets of longan meat.

Loofah is a type of gourd with a woody, earthy flavour often used in soups. Any type of squash may be used as a substitute.

Lotus seeds are most commonly eaten in desserts. Most lotus seeds are sold with the bitter central core or endosperm already removed (if so, the seeds will have a narrow slit on both sides). Sometimes, there are a few rogues with the cores still intact, so check and if you see a dark greenish centre at the top of the seed, split it open and flick out the core. Dried lotus seeds may be stored in an airtight container in the cupboard; they keep for many months.

Fresh yellow wheat noodles (Hokkien *mee*)

Fresh flat rice noodles (*kway teow*)

Fresh laksa noodles (*rice noodles*)

Dried rice vermicelli (*beehoon*)

Dried glass noodles (*tanghoon*)

Noodles are a universal favourite in Singapore which the Malays, Nonyas and Indians have enthusiastically adopted from the Chinese. Both fresh and dried noodles made from either wheat, rice or mung bean flour are found. **Fresh yellow wheat noodles** (Hokkien *mee*) are heavy, spaghetti-like noodles made from wheat flour and egg. Substitute dried ramen or spaghetti. **Fresh flat rice noodles** (*kway teow*) are ribbon-like noodles about 1 cm (½ in) wide, used in soups or fried. Substitute dried rice stick noodles. **Fresh laksa noodles** are round like white spaghetti, but are made from rice flour and traditionally served in laksa soups.

Substitute spaghetti. **Dried rice vermicelli** (*beehoon*) are very fine rice threads that must be plunged into boiling water to soften before use. **Dried glass noodles** (*tang hoon*), made from mung beans, are fine white strands that are generally used in soups. They are also called "cellophane" or "transparent" noodles, both accurate descriptions of their appearance after soaking. Both fresh and dried noodles should be blanched in boiling water before cooking to rinse and revive them—use a pair of long chopsticks to keep them from sticking together.

Mustard seeds are either brownish-black (above right) or yellow (above left). Brown-black mustard seeds are more common in southern Indian cuisine as they impart a nutty flavour to dishes.

Nutmeg is the inner kernel of the fruit of the nutmeg tree. The lacy covering on the nutmeg is another spice—mace. Always grate whole nutmeg just before using as the powdered spice loses its fragrance quickly. Whole nutmegs keep almost indefinitely.

Oyster sauce is the rich, thick and dark extract of dried oysters. It is added to stir-fried vegetable and meat dishes, and must be refrigerated once the bottle is opened. Expensive versions made with abalone and vegetarian versions made from mushrooms are also available. Check the ingredients listed on the bottle as many brands are loaded with MSG.

Palm sugar is sold as a solid block or cylinder of sugar made from the sap of the coconut or arenga sugar palm. It varies in colour from gold to light brown and has a faint caramel taste. To measure, hard palm sugar should be shaved, grated or melted in a microwave oven. Substitute dark brown sugar.

Pandanus leaves impart a subtle fragrance and a green hue to dishes. They are usually tied in a knot and then added to a liquid recipe. Bottled pandanus extract can be substituted in desserts, but if fresh or dried pandanus leaves are not available, omit them from savoury dishes. Vanilla essence may be substituted in dessert recipes.

Persimmons are orange-coloured fruits about the size and shape of a tomato. They are native to China and can be found in most Asian food stores. Be aware that there are two types of persimmons: one type that is eaten when the flesh is pulpy and soft, and another that is eaten when it is firm on the outside and crisp and crunchy on the inside. Both types may be used in the recipes in this book.

Plum Sauce is a sweet and sour reddish-brown condiment made from plums, vinegar and sugar. Sold in jars or cans in Chinese stores.

Prawn crackers or *keropok* are dried wafers made from tapioca starch mixed with bits of prawn or fish, which are deep-fried until crispy and served as a garnish or snack. The wafers must be thoroughly dried before deep-frying them in oil for a few seconds, when they puff up spectacularly. Store fried *keropok* in an airtight container.

Preserved Chinese cabbage, also known as *tang chai*, consists of beige-brown bits of dried salted and seasoned Chinese (Napa) cabbage. These are sold in plastic or cellophane packs and are used as a flavouring, mainly in soups and noodle dishes.

Preserved salted mustard cabbage (*kiam chye*) is used in some Chinese and Nonya dishes. Soak the heavily salted cabbage in water for 15 minutes to remove some of the saltiness, repeating if necessary. This pickled vegetable has a taste similar to sauerkraut, which may be substituted in a pinch.

Preserved salted radish or *chai poh* is a type of dried pickled Japanese radish or daikon. Often added to dishes for its crunchy texture and salty flavour, it keeps almost indefinitely and is available at Asian markets. The Japanese version of pickled daikon may be substituted.

Rice flour is ground from uncooked rice grains. It is used to make Asian desserts in the same way wheat flour is used for Western desserts. Fresh rice flour was traditionally made by soaking the rice overnight and then slowly grinding it in a stone mill. The same result may be achieved by grinding soaked rice in a blender. Rice flour is sold in powdered form in packets in supermarkets and Asian speciality shops.

Rice vinegar is the type of vinegar most commonly used in Singapore cooking. Some recipes call for Chinese black vinegar or red vinegar, both of which have distinctive flavours and are not interchangeable. Balsamic vinegar may be used as a substitute.

Rice wine is added to some marinades and stir-fried dishes in very much the same way that sherry is used in Western cooking. Substitute Japanese sake or dry sherry. **Shaoxing rice wine** is a Chinese yellow rice wine fermented from sticky glutinous rice, yeast and water. A finely aged shaoxing rice wine can be expensive, and can release the fruity flavours of a sweet Muscat wine. Some inferior qualities may taste chemical and almost vinegary. Available in most Asian stores and investing in a better quality shaoxing wine will enhance your cooking. A good sherry or mirin can be substituted.

Sago pearls are dried beads of sago starch obtained by grinding the pith of the sago palm tree to a paste and then pressing it through a sieve. The pearls are glutinous, with little taste, and are used in Asian desserts. Sago pearls must be rinsed in water and drained to remove some of the starch before use. They are sold in various sizes and colours. Available in plastic packets in Asian grocery stores.

Salted fermented soybean paste or *tau cheo* is a seasoning similar to Japanese miso. The paste is sold in jars and varies from dark brown to light golden in colour, and is sometimes labelled "yellow bean sauce". The basic salted soybean paste contains only soybeans, water and salt, however many sweetened versions, or those with added chilli are also common.

Sesame seeds come in black and white varieties; the latter are more common. Sesame seeds are usually dry-roasted over low heat in a pan before use. **Sesame oil** is extracted from roasted (darker oil) or raw (lighter oil) sesame seeds. It is added to Chinese dishes in small quantities as a final touch for its strong nutty flavour and delicate fragrance. It is never used on its own as a frying medium as high heat turns it bitter.

Sour plums are whole beige plums sold in jars of pickling liquid, used for making drinks or flavouring soups and steamed items.

Soy sauce is a fermented sauce brewed from soybeans, water, wheat and salt. **Regular** or **light soy sauce** is very salty and used as a table dip and cooking seasoning. **Dark soy sauce** is denser and less salty and adds a smoky flavour to dishes. **Sweet black soy sauce** is a thick soy sauce brewed with molasses and sugar. if you cannot obtain it, use dark Chinese soy sauce and add brown sugar to sweeten it. **Sweet Indonesian soy sauce** (*kecap manis*) is much sweeter and thicker than normal soy sauce. It has palm sugar and cane molasses added. Sweet Chinese soy sauce may be substituted or you can just add dark brown sugar to normal soy, or you can try to find Indonesian *kecap manis* if you can, because it has a distinctive flavour.

Star anise is a brown, star-shaped spice with eight points, each containing a shiny seed that has a pronounced aniseed flavour. Often used whole and cooked with beef, it is available in plastic packets in the spice section of Asian markets and well-stocked supermarkets.

Tamarind pulp is the fruit pulp found inside the tamarind tree seed pod. It is sold dried in packets or jars and generally still has some seeds and pod fibres mixed in with the dried pulp. It is used as a souring agent in many dishes. To obtain tamarind juice, mash the pulp in warm water, strain and discard the seeds or fibres. If using already cleaned tamarind pulp, slightly reduce the amounts called for in the recipes. Dried tamarind pulp keeps indefinitely in an airtight container.

Firm tofu

Pressed tofu *(tau kwa)*

Soft tofu

Dried sweet tofu

Tofu skin

Tofu, or bean curd, is available in various textures ranging from silken to firm. **Firm tofu** holds its shape when cut or cooked and has a stronger, slightly sour taste. **Pressed tofu** *(tau kwa)* (which confusingly is often labelled as "firm tofu") has much of the moisture extracted and is therefore much firmer in texture than normal tofu—it is commonly eaten in Asia as a meat substitute. **Soft** or **silken tofu** is slippery and tends to crumble easily, but has a silky texture and refined flavour. Soft tofu is available packed in square plastic boxes or shaped into cylinders and wrapped in plastic. Another type of tofu sometimes added to braised dishes or soups is **dried deep-fried tofu** *(tau pok)*, which is generally sold in small rectangles. These are often sold on strings in Asia, but are elsewhere usually packed in plastic. They are light and spongy in texture, and need to be dipped briefly in boiling water to remove the oil before being used. Dried deep-fried tofu has an almost nutty flavour and is particularly appreciated for the way it soaks up the liquid to which it is added. It can be kept refrigerated for at least two weeks. **Dried sweet tofu strips** *(tau kee)* are chewy and only slightly sweet. They are brown in colour and are often used in vegetarian cooking as a meat substitute. **Tofu Skin** is the thin layer of soy protein that forms on top of soybean milk when it is boiled. The skin is skimmed off and dried. It is sold in sheets as a wrapper. It has little flavour but a wonderful texture. It is to be moistened with a wet cloth before use. It is a widely-used ingredient in vegetarian foods as it is a good and healthy alternative to meat. Tofu skin can be deep fried, steamed or even used as a garnish. Tofu skin wrappers are also made from **dried tofu skin** and are large, folded, opaque sheets that are light brown in colour and often used to wrap spring rolls and other fillings. Tofu skin is available in plastic packets in Asian markets and the various forms of tofu can be found in any well-stocked supermarket.

Turmeric *(kunyit)* is a root similar to ginger but with a bright yellow to orange colour and a strong woody flavour. Turmeric has antiseptic and astringent qualities, and stains permanently, so scrub your knife blade, hands and chopping board immediately after handling. Purchase fresh turmeric root as needed as the flavour fades after a few days. Substitute 1 teaspoon ground turmeric for 1 in (2.5 cm) of the fresh root. **Turmeric leaves** are the large leaves of the turmeric plant that are used in some parts of Asia for cooking. They can also be thinly sliced and eaten with Nasi Ulam (page 59) and are seldom available outside Asia.

Water chestnuts are roots about the size of chestnuts. They are crunchy, white and juicy-sweet inside. Peel the dark brown skins before eating. It is worth the effort to use fresh water chestnuts if you can find them. Their crisp texture and sweet flavour make them popular in salads, stir-fried vegetable dishes and desserts. Store refrigerated, immersed in water, for up to a week.

Wild ginger bud *(bunga kantan)* are the pink buds of the wild ginger plant, also known as torch ginger. They are highly aromatic and lend a distinct fragrance to dishes of Malay and Nonya origin. Available in Asian markets.

White fungus *(suet yee)* or white woodears, have a crunchy texture and a slightly sweet flavour. They look like sponges and will expand into frilly white clouds when soaked in water. They are used for their appealingly resilient texture. They are sold dried and must be soaked in water before using.

Wonton wrappers are made from wheat dough, and come in a variety of sizes and thicknesses. They are filled with meat or vegetables, then steamed, fried or used in soups. Fresh or frozen wonton wrappers are available in most supermarkets.

Yew char kway or *yutiao* (Chinese crullers) are 2 long sticks of dough stuck together and then deep-fried. They are savoury rather than sweet and are traditionally eaten with rice porridge (congee). Available in Asian fresh markets.

Marinades, Chutneys, Sambals and Achars

Hoisin, Wine and Sesame Marinade

This sauce is ideal for marinating pork or chicken (whole or cut into pieces) before roasting.

Makes 115 ml (scant ½ cup)
Preparation time: 5 mins

1 tablespoon hoisin sauce
4 tablespoons Shaoxing rice wine
1 tablespoon sesame oil
1 tablespoon minced garlic
1 teaspoon ground black pepper
1 tablespoon dark soy sauce

1 In a bowl, combine the ingredients until well blended.

Hoisin and Worcestershire Sauce Marinade

We like to use this sauce to marinate barbecued spareribs or fried chicken.

Makes 100 ml (scant ½ cup)
Preparation time: 5 mins

2 tablespoons hoisin sauce
2 tablespoons oyster sauce
1 tablespoon Worcestershire sauce
2 tablespoons water

1 In a bowl, combine the ingredients until well blended.

Chilli, Lime and Peanut Brittle Dip

This dip—ideal for spring rolls and fried foods—is Terry's original blend of Thai, Vietnamese and Cantonese influences.

Serves 2–3
Preparation time: 5 mins

4 red finger-length chillies
2 tablespoons fresh lime juice
1 tablespoon fish sauce
3 tablespoons crushed peanut brittle
1 teaspoon sugar

1 Deseed and finely chop the chillies. Mix well with all the remaining ingredients.

Red Coconut Chutney

We pair this fiery red chutney with South Indian breads and rice dishes.

Serves 3–4
Cooking time: 30 seconds
Preparation time: 10 mins

5 dried red finger-length chillies
1 cup (100 g) freshly grated coconut
3 Asian shallots, finely sliced
1 tablespoon chopped fresh ginger root
½ teaspoon salt
¼ teaspoon sugar
2 tablespoons oil
1 teaspoon black mustard seeds
3 sprigs curry leaves, stalk discarded

1 Deseed 4 of the dried chillies and soak them in warm water for 10 minutes. Drain, reserving the water, then combine 2 tablespoons of the reserved water with the grated coconut, shallots, ginger, salt and sugar in a blender. Blend to a thick paste, then transfer to a heatproof bowl.

2 Heat the oil in a small pan over medium-high heat. When hot, add the mustard seeds, curry leaves and the remaining dried chilli. Stir-fry for 20 seconds, then pour them over the coconut mixture and stir to mix well. Serve immediately. Consume within a day as it won't keep.

Sweet Pineapple Relish

This warm sweet-and-spicy relish is a real treat with grilled chicken and seafood dishes.

Makes approximately 500 g (1 lb)
Cooking time: 5 mins
Preparation time: 10 mins

2 tablespoons dried prawn paste (*belachan*)
4 red finger-length chillies, deseeded and finely chopped
2 teaspoons sugar
1 fresh pineapple, about 500 g (1 lb)
1 tablespoon oil

1 Roast the dried prawn paste over an open flame for 3 minutes. Grind together with the chillies and sugar in a blender until very fine.

2 Skin the pineapple and quarter lengthwise. Remove and discard the central hard core and slice the rest into cubes about 1 cm (⅜ in) thick.

3 Heat the oil in a wok over high heat and fry the pineapple for 1–2 minutes. Remove from the heat and chop coarsely. Mix well with the dried prawn paste and serve immediately.

Cucumber Onion Raita

Though there are countless types of Indian raitas, all are based on a combination of raw vegetables and yoghurt. Here, cucumber amplifies the dish's cooling characteristics.

Serves 2–3
Preparation time: 5 mins

1 Japanese or baby cucumber
1 small onion, peeled and sliced into thin rings
2 teaspoons salt
1 cup (250 ml) thick plain yoghurt
1 tablespoon fresh lime juice

1 Peel the cucumber and quarter it lengthwise, then slice into thin quarter-moons. Mix with the onion rings and sprinkle with salt. Set aside for 20 minutes, then drain, squeezing lightly to remove some juice and rinse well with cold water.

2 Mix the vegetables with the yoghurt and lime juice. Serve alongside curries and biryanis.

Basic Garam Masala Spice Mix

This Indian spice mix should be fragrant and compelling—which is why the coriander and cumin seeds are roasted whole before grinding, producing a heightened aroma.

Makes 125 g (½ cup)
Preparation time: 5 mins

3 tablespoons coriander seeds
2 tablespoons cumin seeds
2 teaspoons black peppercorns
1 teaspoon ground cardamom
1 teaspoon ground cinnamon
1 teaspoon ground cloves
1 teaspoon ground nutmeg

1 Set a wok (preferably non-stick) over low heat. When hot, dry-fry the coriander seeds for 4–6 minutes, stirring continuously, until they are fragrant and have very slightly darkened. Transfer to a bowl.

2 Dry-fry the cumin seeds for 2–3 minutes until fragrant.

3 When both spices have cooled, grind them in a spice grinder with the black peppercorns until fine. Add all the remaining spices and stir to mix. Store in an airtight jar in a dark, dry place.

Rice Wine, Oyster Sauce and Ginger Marinade

This versatile sauce works great as a marinade for steamed chicken, as a base for braising pork or as a sauce for stir-fried meat or liver.

Makes 180 ml (¾ cup)
Preparation time: 5 mins

4 tablespoons Shaoxing rice wine
2 tablespoons oyster sauce
2 tablespoons sesame oil
1 tablespoon minced fresh ginger root
3 tablespoons water

1 In a bowl, combine the ingredients until well blended.

Fermented Tofu, Shallots and Lime Juice

This typical Chinese side dish is eaten with rice porridge. You can also use white fermented tofu (*foo yee*), which has a milder flavour.

Serves 2–3
Preparation time: 2 mins

3 squares fermented red tofu (*lam yee*)
5 Asian shallots, finely sliced
2 tablespoons fresh lime juice
1 teaspoon sugar

1 Lightly mash the fermented tofu until well blended. Gently mix in all the remaining ingredients. Serve with porridge or rice and other bland fried dishes.

Pickled Green Papaya

Crunchy and cool, this pickle is equally good paired with spicy curries or cold meats, or eaten on its own as a snack.

Makes approximately 600 g (1⅓ lbs) pickle
Preparation time: 20 mins, plus 40 mins standing time

1 firm green (unripe) papaya, about 700 g (1½ lbs)
2 teaspoons salt
2 cups (500 ml) distilled white vinegar
100 g (½ cup) fine granulated sugar

1 Skin the papaya and halve lengthwise. Scrape out the white seeds and discard. With a vegetable peeler, shave the papaya flesh into long thin strips. Transfer to a large bowl, sprinkle with the salt and toss to mix well. Set aside for 40 minutes.

2 Squeeze as much of the moisture out of the papaya as possible. Pack the papaya strips into a large, very clean screwtop jar.

3 Dissolve the sugar in the vinegar over low heat. Let cool slightly, then pour over the papaya strips. When completely cool, cover tightly. Let steep at least two days before serving. Pickle keeps for a couple of weeks in the refrigerator.

Seafood Curry Powder

Curry powder should keep for up to three months. If you live in a humid, tropical climate, always check for any mould before using—mouldy powder will have a musty, unpleasant smell.

Makes about 250 g (1 cup)
Cooking time: 10–15 mins

150 g (¾ cup) coriander seeds
6 tablespoons cumin seeds
3 tablespoons fennel seeds
2–3 teaspoons cardamom pods
1 teaspoon fenugreek seeds
½ star anise pod
1 teaspoon cloves
2 tablespoons ground black pepper
2 tablespoons ground red pepper
2 tablespoons ground turmeric

1 Dry-roast the whole spices individually, over a very low heat, until they become fragrant. Set aside and when they have cooled, grind them together.

2 Combine the ground spices with the pepper, ground red pepper and turmeric. Dry-roast the mixture in a non-stick wok over low heat, stirring continuously and thoroughly, for about 10–15 minutes, until the spices start to release their aromatic oils. Do not let them scorch. When done, transfer to a bowl, and when cool, store in airtight jars in a dark, dry place.

Chilli, Soybean and Lime Dip

This salty and savoury dip goes great with steamed and boiled seafood.

Serves 2–4
Preparation time: 5 mins

3 tablespoons salted fermented soybean paste (*tau cheo*) or miso
2 red finger-length chillies, deseeded and finely sliced
5 Asian shallots, finely sliced
1½ tablespoons fresh lime juice or 1 tablespoon distilled white vinegar
1 teaspoon sugar

1 Spoon the soybean paste into a small bowl. Drain and discard most of the salty preserving liquid. Roughly mash the beans and stir in the chillies and shallots, followed by the lime juice and sugar. Stir until the sugar completely dissolves.

Meat Curry Powder

This curry powder, and the seafood variation that follows, are not difficult to make if you have access to good quality whole spices and a good spice grinder. Purchase each spice whole and dry-roast them individually until they become very fragrant. When they have cooled, grind them together, then store them in an airtight jar or in the freezer. Blend wet aromatics like ginger, garlic and onions with the curry powder to a smooth paste, to be fried in oil before adding your meat or seafood and other ingredients.

Makes about 250 g (1 cup)
Cooking time: 10–15 mins

200 g (1 cup) coriander seeds
7 tablespoons cumin seeds
3½ tablespoons fennel seeds
2–3 teaspoons cardamom pods
1 teaspoon cloves
½ small stick cinnamon
2 tablespoons ground black pepper
2 tablespoons ground red pepper
2 tablespoons ground turmeric

1 Dry-roast the whole spices individually, over a very low heat, until they become fragrant. Set aside and when they have cooled, grind them together with the cinnamon.

2 Combine the ground spices with the pepper, ground red pepper and turmeric.

3 Set a wok (preferably non-stick, or very well seasoned) over low heat. When the wok is hot, add the mixture and dry-fry, stirring continuously and thoroughly, for about 10–15 minutes, until the spices start to release their aromatic oils. Do not let them scorch. When done, transfer to a bowl, and when cool, store in airtight jars in a dark, dry place.

Dried Prawns, Chilli, Lime and Mint Dip

Ground dried prawns—the best you can buy, please—are delicious in chilli-based dips. This makes a good base for a cucumber or pineapple side salad or kerabu; just mix a few spoonfuls with the chopped fruit.

Serves 2–3
Preparation time: 10 mins plus 30 mins soaking time

3 tablespoons dried prawns
4 red finger-length chillies
4 tablespoons fresh lime juice
2 teaspoons sugar
1 teaspoon fish sauce
1 teaspoon finely chopped mint leaves
2 tablespoons water

1 Soak the dried prawns in hot water for 30 minutes until soft. Drain thoroughly.

2 Grind the dried prawns in a blender until fine. Add the chillies and grind until well blended. Stir in all the remaining ingredients. Serve immediately.

Pickled Green Chillies

These pickled chillies are great to have on hand when you want a quick bite of something to stimulate your palate. A few of these pickles will add new excitement to your favourite hot or cold sandwiches.

Makes 1 large jar pickled chillies
Cooking time: 3 mins
Preparation time: 10 mins

20 green finger-length chillies, washed, stalks discarded
2 cups (500 ml) distilled white vinegar
½ teaspoon salt
2 teaspoons sugar

1 Slice the chillies diagonally, about 6 mm (¼ in) thick.

2 Bring the vinegar to a boil with the salt and sugar over high heat. Add the chillies and simmer for 15 seconds. Pour all into a clean screwtop jar. Once cool, cover and store in the fridge.

Roasted Coconut Sambal

A terribly addictive accompaniment, this sambal is served as part of an Indonesian *rijsttafel* or "rice table," and also a Nonya long table meal.

Serves 4–5
Cooking time: 10 mins
Preparation time: 10 mins

3 stalks lemongrass, tender inner part of bottom third only
4 green finger-length chillies
6 Asian shallots
200 g (2 cups) freshly grated coconut
¾ teaspoon salt

1 Finely slice the lemongrass, chillies and shallots. Mix well with the grated coconut and salt.

2 Heat a wok over low flame and dry-fry, stirring constantly, until the coconut and the other ingredients turn an even golden brown, about 10 minutes. Watch the mixture diligently to prevent scorching. Cool completely and store airtight in the fridge; consume within a week.

Satay Peanut Sauce

This spicy peanut sauce is the classic accompaniment for grilled meat or chicken satay, a popular Indonesian specialty that has spread to Singapore, South-East Asia and beyond.

Serves 4–6
Cooking time: 15 mins
Preparation time: 15 mins

1½ tablespoons tamarind pulp
1¼ cups (300 ml) water
3 tablespoons oil
1 tablespoon sugar, or to taste
185 g (1¼ cups) roasted unsalted peanuts
200 g (⅔ cup) canned crushed pineapple

Spice Paste
4 dried red finger-length chillies, soaked until soft
10 Asian shallots
2 cloves garlic
½ tablespoon dried prawn paste (*belachan*), dry-roasted
4 candlenuts or macadamia nuts
1 stalk lemongrass, tender inner part of bottom third only, sliced
2 thin slices galangal root

1 Grind all the Spice Paste ingredients together until fine. Mash the tamarind pulp with the water. Strain to obtain the juice, discarding the solids. Pulse the peanuts in the food processor until very finely chopped.

2 Heat the oil in a wok over medium heat and stir-fry the Spice Paste for 5 minutes, until thick and fragrant. Add the tamarind juice and simmer for 10 minutes, then add the sugar and peanuts. Taste and adjust the seasonings. Pour into serving bowls—one for each person—and add a dollop of crushed pineapple to each bowl. Serve the sauce and any extra pineapple on the side, with the satay.

Tamarind and Soy Sauce Marinade

The delicious blend of flavours in this marinade is similar to the famous Filipino *adobo*.

Makes 150 ml (⅔ cup)
Preparation time: 5 mins

2 tablespoons tamarind pulp
6 tablespoons water
2 tablespoons dark soy sauce
1 tablespoon sugar
2 teaspoon ground pepper
1 teaspoon salt

1 Mash the tamarind pulp with the water. Strain to obtain the juice, discarding the solids. Mix the tamarind juice with all the other ingredients, stirring until the sugar completely dissolves.

Chilli, Garlic and Vinegar Dip

This Teochew dip is usually served with soy-braised poultry and pork.

Serves 3–5
Preparation time: 5 mins

6 red finger-length chillies
3 cloves garlic, peeled
5 tablespoons distilled white vinegar
½ teaspoon sugar
½ teaspoon salt

1 Finely mince the chillies and garlic with a cleaver. Mix with the vinegar, sugar and salt. A large batch of this can be made and kept in a screw-top jar, refrigerated, for a few days.

Sambal Belachan with Kaffir Lime Leaf

This is the essential Peranakan sambal, without which a Nonya dining table is naked. To get the right texture for this sambal, it's necessary to grind the ingredients the old-fashioned way—with a mortar and pestle. Sorry, no food processors allowed!

Makes 125 ml (½ cup) sambal
Cooking time: 3 mins
Preparation time: 10 mins

1 tablespoon dried prawn paste (*belachan*)
5 red finger-length chillies, deseeded and sliced
3 bird's-eye chillies, deseeded and sliced
3 kaffir lime leaves, very finely sliced
1 tablespoon hot water
3 tablespoons fresh lime juice

1 Roast the dried prawn paste over an open flame until fragrant, crusty and slightly charred. In a mortar, grind the chillies until fine. Add the dried prawn paste and pound until incorporated, then add the shredded kaffir lime leaves and pound to blend. Mix in the hot water and lime juice. Serve immediately.

Note: To prevent the dried prawn paste odour from permeating the house, wrap it in foil and roast in a low oven or in a dry pan for 4–5 minutes.

Daikon Radish Pickles with Chillies

This classic Cantonese pickle is best served with roast meats.

Makes approximately 500 g (1 lb) pickle
Cooking time: 1 min
Preparation time: 20 mins plus 30 mins standing

1 daikon radish, about 500 g (1 lb)
3 red finger-length chillies
2 teaspoons salt
2 cups (500 ml) distilled white vinegar
75 g (¼ cup) fine granulated sugar

1 Peel the radish and cut it into sticks the size of a little finger. Slice the chillies into large diagonal pieces. Combine in a bowl and sprinkle with the salt. Set aside for 30 minutes.

2 Squeeze as much of the moisture as possible out of the vegetables, then rinse briefly in cold water and squeeze dry again. Pack into a large, very clean screwtop jar.

3 Bring the vinegar and sugar to a boil, then turn off heat and let the mixture cool for 5 minutes. Pour into the jar over the radish and chillies making sure they are completely covered. Let cool completely, then steep overnight, covered, before serving. Keeps for a couple of weeks in the refrigerator.

Sambal Belimbing

This hearty sambal, made with the sour tropical belimbing fruit (see page 13) and fresh prawns, can be enjoyed as light meal when served with rice.

Serves 4–5
Cooking time: 16 mins
Preparation time: 20 mins plus 20 mins standing time

4–5 belimbing fruits, sliced into thin discs
2 tablespoons salt
6 tablespoons oil
4 cloves garlic, thinly sliced
2 stalks lemongrass, tender inner part of bottom third only, thinly sliced
150 g (5 oz) fresh prawns, peeled
1 cup (250 ml) thick coconut milk
2 teaspoons sugar
Salt to taste

Spice Paste
1 tablespoon dried prawn paste (*belachan*), dry-roasted
4 red finger-length chillies
1 small onion, peeled and sliced

1 Cut each belimbing into 6-mm (¼-in) thick slices. Sprinkle with the salt and set aside for 20 minutes. Very gently squeeze the belimbing with your hands to remove the moisture, transfer to a clean bowl, then rinse well with cold water. Drain and squeeze again.

2 Grind the Spice Paste ingredients together until fine.

3 Heat the oil in a wok over medium heat. When very hot, stir-fry the garlic and lemongrass for 2–3 minutes until golden and crispy, then transfer to paper towels to drain.

4 In the same oil, stir-fry the Spice Paste for 7–8 minutes, stirring constantly, until fragrant. Add the belimbing, prawns and coconut milk, bring to a simmer and cook for 5–6 minutes more until the belimbing are soft. Add the sugar and salt. Garnish with the fried lemongrass and garlic and serve with hot rice.

Crispy Ikan Bilis with Peanuts

This unique sambal, made with dried baby anchovies and peanuts, is served with Nasi Lemak (page 52) to create a light but protein-packed rice dish. In Malaysia, *nasi lemak* is wrapped in banana leaves and eaten for breakfast. If you fall in love with the flavours of this dish, why not serve it with your favourite meals?

Serves 4–6
Cooking time: 16 mins
Preparation time: 20 mins

Oil, for deep-frying
6 tablespoons raw peanuts
200 g (7 oz) dried *ikan bilis* (baby anchovies), cleaned
1 tablespoon tamarind pulp
4 tablespoons water
4 tablespoons oil
¼ teaspoon salt
1 tablespoon sugar
1 tablespoon tomato paste

Spice Paste
3 red finger-length chillies
1 small onion, sliced
4 cloves garlic
1 teaspoon dried prawn paste (*belachan*), dry-roasted

1 Heat the oil in a wok over medium-low heat until it ripples under the surface, but there is no haze, about 140°C (275°F). Add the peanuts and fry, stirring frequently, for about 4 minutes or until golden (scrape the skin off one peanut to check). Remove from the oil with a slotted spoon and drain on paper towels.

2 Spread the *ikan bilis* on a plate and microwave on high for 1¼ minutes to make sure it is very dry. (Alternatively, dry in the sun for a while.) Return the oil to frying temperature, add the *ikan bilis* and fry for 4–5 minutes until crisp and golden brown. Drain well on paper towels.

3 Grind all the Spice Paste ingredients together until fine.

4 Mash the tamarind pulp with the water and strain to obtain the juice, discarding the solids.

5 Heat 4 tablespoons of fresh oil in a clean wok over medium-high heat and stir-fry the Spice Paste for 6 minutes until fragrant and thick. Add the tamarind juice, salt, sugar and tomato paste. Stir to blend well. Bring to a quick boil, add the *ikan bilis* and peanuts and mix well, then serve.

Fried Chilli Sambal

This basic, all-purpose sambal is a staple in our kitchen. You can serve it with most meals, especially with dishes like *nasi lemak, laksa,* Hokkien mee and *mee siam.* You can also use it to marinate chicken or seafood such as prawns and meaty fish before grilling or barbecuing. As always, increase the chillies if you like more heat.

Makes approximately 500 g (1 lb) sambal
Cooking time: 12 mins
Preparation time: 10 mins

6 cloves garlic
4 candlenuts or macadamia nuts
3 small onions
8–10 dried red finger-length chillies, soaked until soft
2 tablespoons tamarind pulp
¾ cup (200 ml) water
6 tablespoons oil
2 tablespoons tomato paste
1 teaspoon salt
1 tablespoon sugar

1 Grind the garlic, candlenuts, onions and chillies until very fine. If the paste is very dry, add a little water to obtain a moist but not soggy texture.

2 Mash the tamarind pulp with the water. Strain to obtain the juice, discarding the solids.

3 Heat the oil in a wok over low heat. When very hot, add the paste and stir-fry for about 10 minutes, stirring constantly, until the paste is thick and shiny with oil—this indicates the raw spices are adequately cooked.

4 Add the tomato paste, salt, sugar and ¾ of the tamarind juice. Stir well, then add the salt and sugar. Add the remaining tamarind juice. Stir-fry for 1 more minute, then transfer the contents to a clean bowl or jar. When cool, seal in an airtight container and store in the fridge. This keeps for a few weeks.

Sweet Mango Chutney

Combining sweetness and heat, this famous chutney is a perfect accompaniment to curried dishes. If you can't find green mangoes, you may substitute ripe mangoes. In that case, add half the amount of sugar (adding more if needed after tasting) and add the mango pieces to the wok last, cooking them for only 1 minute.

Makes 1 jar chutney
Cooking time: 13 mins
Preparation time: 15 mins

3 small green mangoes or 2 medium-sized ones, peeled, halved and stone removed
3 dried red finger-length chillies, deseeded and soaked until soft
2 tablespoons oil
1 teaspoon salt
1 tablespoon finely chopped fresh ginger root
½ teaspoon Basic Garam Masala Spice Mix (page 23)
1 tablespoon raisins or sultanas
½ cup (125 ml) vinegar
2 tablespoons water
1 teaspoon ground cumin
4 cloves garlic, thinly sliced
45 g (¼ cup) brown or demerara sugar

1 Cut each mango half into two pieces lengthwise, then again crosswise, so each half yields four pieces.

2 Drain the chillies and pat dry. Heat the oil in a wok over medium heat and stir-fry the chillies for about 45 seconds, until almost brown and slightly puffy. Add the salt, ginger and Basic Garam Masala Spice Mix. Stir-fry for about 2 minutes over low heat. Add the mangoes and remaining ingredients and cook for 8–10 minutes or until the mango is tender but not mushy.

3 Remove from the heat and let the chutney cool thoroughly before transferring to a clean glass jar. Cover tightly and refrigerate for at least one day (preferably three to four days) before consuming.

Kerabu Cucumber Salad

Grated coconut and a classic spice paste give this cucumber salad an unmistakably Singaporean twist.

Serves 2–3 Cooking time: 5 mins
Preparation time: 10 mins plus 40 mins standing time

1 small cucumber
½ teaspoon salt
3 tablespoons freshly grated coconut
2 tablespoons fresh lime juice
1 teaspoon sugar

Spice Paste
2 tablespoons dried prawns
4 Asian shallots
4 cloves garlic
3 red finger-length chillies

1 To make the Spice Paste, soak the dried prawns in warm water until soft, about 40 minutes, then drain and grind with the shallots, garlic and chillies until fine.

2 Peel the cucumber and quarter it lengthwise. Remove the seeds and soft core, then slice the firm flesh diagonally into diamond shapes about 6 mm (¼ in) thick. Sprinkle with salt and set aside.

3 Dry-fry the grated coconut in a non-stick skillet over medium heat for 3–5 minutes, stirring constantly, until lightly browned.

4 Drain the cucumber of any juices, then toss with the Spice Paste, fried coconut, lime juice and sugar. Serve immediately.

Nonya Achar

These pickled vegetables take some work and time, but they keep for months in the refrigerator. Sun-dry the vegetables if you can; alternatively, dry them in an oven at very low heat.

Makes 1¾ kg (3¾ lbs) pickle
Cooking time: 25 mins
Preparation time: 40 mins plus drying time

1 cucumber
1 carrot
180 g (6 oz) Chinese (Napa) cabbage
125 g (4 oz) cauliflower
½ tablespoon sea salt
2 cups (500 ml) distilled white vinegar
1 cup (250 ml) water
10 Asian shallots, peeled
10 cloves garlic, peeled
3 tablespoons oil
1 tablespoon sugar
2 tablespoons sesame seeds, lightly roasted
100 g (⅔ cup) finely chopped roasted peanuts

Spice Paste
18 Asian shallots
75 g (2½ oz) ginger, peeled
5 dried red finger-length chillies, deseeded and soaked until soft
30 g (1 oz) fresh turmeric root, peeled

1 Peel the cucumbers and halve them lengthwise. Scrape out the core, taking care to remove every bit of the soft centre or the cucumber may rot before it dries. Cut the cucumber and carrot into thick 5-cm (2-in) lengths and slice the cabbage into 2-cm (¾-in) wide strips. Separate the cauliflower into small florets.

2 Spread the vegetables out on a large tray and sprinkle with salt. Let stand in the sun for two days, until they are dry to the touch and just slightly shriveled.

3 Bring the vinegar and water to a boil in a deep pot. Blanch the vegetables, shallots and garlic, a small batch at a time, until they plump up again—it should take only several seconds per batch. Remove with a slotted spoon and transfer to a clean bowl. There should be very little liquid left at the end.

4 Grind all the Spice Paste ingredients together until fine. Heat the oil in a wok over medium heat and stir-fry the Spice Paste until fragrant, 7–8 minutes. Toss well with the remaining blanching liquid, vegetables, sugar, sesame seeds and peanuts. Transfer to two sterilised or very clean, dry screwtop jars. Store in the fridge; let stand at least three days before serving as a side dish.

Snacks, Soups and Salads

Curry Puffs

Old-fashioned Indian curry puffs used to be shaped from handmade puff pastry, rich with margarine and baked in diesel-fired clay ovens. We use store-bought puff pastry made with butter because it isn't laden with hydrogenated fat and, we admit, for its great convenience.

Makes 8–9 curry puffs Cooking time: 25 mins
Preparation time: 30 mins

5 tablespoons oil
250 g (1½ cups) ground lamb or beef
3 potatoes, boiled, peeled and diced
1 cup (250 ml) water
1 teaspoon salt
1 kg (2 lbs) frozen puff pastry
2 hard-boiled eggs, chunkily diced
2 eggs, beaten

Spice Paste
3 tablespoons Meat Curry Powder (page 24)
1 small onion, sliced
5 cloves garlic
2 tablespoons chopped fresh ginger root
2–3 dried red finger-length chillies,
   soaked until soft
1 tablespoon water

1 Preheat the oven to 200°C (400°F). Grind all the Spice Paste ingredients together in a blender until very fine.

2 Heat the oil in a wok over medium heat and stir-fry the Spice Paste until fragrant and thick, 5–6 minutes. Add the mutton or beef and fry for 2 minutes, then add the cooked diced potatoes, water and salt. Continue to fry, stirring frequently, until the liquid has evaporated and the curry is thick, 6–7 minutes. Remove from the heat and let cool completely.

3 Roll out the puff pastry so it is 3 mm (⅛ in) thick. Cut into 15-cm (6-in) squares. Place 1 heaping tablespoon of the filling across a diagonal half of a square and top with some boiled egg pieces. Fold the pastry diagonally over the filling to make a triangle and seal the edges with some beaten egg. Brush the top with more beaten egg to glaze. Repeat with the remaining pastry and filling.

4 Transfer the curry puffs to a greased baking tray and bake at 200°C (400°F) for 10–12 minutes or until well browned. Serve warm.

Otak Otak

This is a classic Singapore snack—an intoxicating blend of fish, spices and fragrant herbs ground together to form a pâté and then grilled over charcoal in fragrant banana or palm leaves. Eat with *nasi lemak* or make sandwiches with it on buttered crusty bread.

Serves 4–5   Cooking time: 10 mins
Preparation time: 25 mins

3 kaffir lime leaves, very thinly sliced
Small handful laksa leaves (*daun kesom* or Vietnamese mint),
    thinly sliced
1 teaspoon salt
1 teaspoon sugar
750 g (1⅔ lbs) deboned mackerel meat or other oily fish
3 eggs, lightly beaten
2 tablespoons oil
¾ cup (200 ml) thick coconut milk
6–8 banana leaf or aluminium squares, each about 25 cm (10 in)

Spice Paste
2 small onions
8 candlenuts or macadamia nuts
8–12 dried red finger-length chillies, soaked until soft
2 tablespoons ground coriander
1 tablespoon dried prawn paste (*belachan*), dry-roasted
3 slices galangal root
2 stalks lemongrass, tender inner part of bottom third only,
    thinly sliced

1 Grind all the Spice Paste ingredients together until fine. Mix with the kaffir lime leaves, laksa leaves, salt and sugar.

2 Grind the fish meat in a food processor to a slightly coarse paste. Transfer to a bowl and add the eggs, oil and Spice Paste. Stir with a spoon in one direction only. Slowly mix in the coconut milk. The finished paste should have a consistency like softened butter.

3 Scald the banana leaves in boiling water to soften and then drain well. Place 2–3 tablespoons of the fish mixture in the centre of each square, spreading it to about 6 mm (¼ in) thick. Fold the edges of the leaf over the filling. Secure the ends with toothpicks, weaving them through the leaf layers (like pinning pieces of fabric together).

4 Cook under a broiler or over hot charcoal for 8–10 minutes, turning once halfway through. Serve hot. Unwrap at the table.

Note: An oily fish is needed to stand up to the spices. Chris has made this with a mix of trout and mackerel, cutting back on the spice paste slightly, with great success.

Bergedel Potato Fish Cakes

The Dutch colonisation of Indonesia created many fascinating hybrid dishes. Danish *frikadeller* meatballs were transformed into *bergedel*, ground meat and potato balls now an essential part of any *nasi padang* (rice and cooked food) stall's repertoire. Terry's version uses fish, which makes them similar to the fish cutlets of Sri Lanka, itself once colonised by the Portuguese … but that's another story.

Serves 6–8 Cooking time: 45 mins
Preparation time: 20 mins

4 large or 6 medium potatoes (about 750 g/1⅔ lbs total)
3 tablespoons oil
2 tablespoons chopped onion
1 tablespoon minced garlic
250 g (2 cups) flaked cooked fish
1 teaspoon ground black pepper
1 teaspoon salt
½ teaspoon ground cloves
Oil, for deep-frying
4 tablespoons plain flour
2 eggs, beaten

1 Cook the potatoes in boiling water for 16–20 minutes (or microwave on high) until soft. Drain very well and peel, then mash finely in a large mixing bowl.

2 Heat the oil in a wok over medium heat and stir-fry the onion and garlic for 5–6 minutes or until softened and lightly browned. Add them to the mashed potatoes along with the fish, pepper, salt and clove, and mix until well blended.

3 Heat the oil in a wok over medium heat. With well-floured hands, roll egg-sized balls of mashed potato mixture and form them into round, slightly flattened patties. Dust each patty lightly with flour, then coat well with the beaten egg and slip into the hot oil. Deep-fry in batches, for 3–5 minutes per batch, turning once, until golden brown. Drain well on paper towels and serve hot.

Note: You can use any white fish—even drained water-packed canned tuna, in a pinch.

Crab Cakes

Enhanced with the exotic flavours of lemongrass and kaffir lime leaves, these tasty little morsels are quite different from their American cousins.

Serves 6–8 Cooking time: 6–10 mins
Preparation time: 15 mins

650g (5½ cups) cooked crabmeat
2 kaffir lime leaves, very thinly sliced
2 eggs, lightly beaten
½ teaspoon salt
3 tablespoons plain flour
Oil, for deep-frying
Sliced cucumbers, to garnish
Sweet bottled chilli sauce, to serve

Spice Paste
2 small onions
4–6 dried red finger-length chillies, soaked until soft
1 tablespoon ground coriander
1 teaspoon dried prawn paste (*belachan*), dry-roasted
1 stalk lemongrass, tender inner part of bottom third only, thinly sliced

1 Grind all the Spice Paste ingredients until fine.

2 Mix the Spice Paste, crabmeat, kaffir lime leaves, beaten egg, salt and flour together until well blended. Scoop heaping tablespoons of the mixture and pat into small cakes about 12 mm (½ in) thick.

3 Heat the oil in a wok over medium heat until shimmering. Deep-fry the crab cakes in batches until golden brown, 2–3 minutes per batch, turning once. Drain on paper towels and serve with the sliced cucumbers and chilli sauce.

Sui Gow Prawn and Crab Dumpling Soup

The dumplings in this soup, a more luxurious version of the plebeian wonton, are served as a snack or side dish by hawkers. *Sui gow* skins are made from wheat dough, and come in a round shape. They are available in Asian markets or supermarkets.

Serves 5–6   Cooking time: 30 mins
Preparation time: 20 mins

5 cups (1.2 litres) water
2 tablespoons *ikan bilis* (dried baby anchovies)
200 g (1 cup) ground pork
125 g (½ cup) ground prawn meat
150 g (1½ cups) cooked crabmeat
2 stalks green onions (scallions), chopped
4 tablespoons soy sauce
1 tablespoon cornstarch
1 teaspoon ground pepper
1½ teaspoons sesame oil
20–25 *sui gow* skins
1 teaspoon cornstarch mixed with
    1 tablespoon water
Chopped green onions (scallions), to garnish

1 Bring the water to a boil, add the *ikan bilis* and simmer for 15 minutes. Strain the stock and discard the *ikan bilis*.

2 Mix the ground pork, prawn, crabmeat, green onions, 1 tablespoon soy sauce, cornstarch, pepper and half the sesame oil together until well blended. Place 1 heaping teaspoon of the mixture on a *sui gow* skin, fold over to make a half-moon shape and seal the edges with a little of the cornstarch mixture. Repeat with the remaining skins and filling.

3 Bring a large pot of water to a boil. Slip in half the *sui gow* and simmer for 5–6 minutes until they are cooked and float up. Drain and transfer to the stock pot. Repeat with the remaining *sui gow*.

4 Add the remaining soy sauce and sesame oil to the stock and reheat until just about to boil. Garnish with green onions and serve immediately.

Fishball and Glass Noodle Soup

This simple clear soup of Malaysian origin can be heated up
to your taste with the addition of sliced red chillies.

Serves 6   Cooking time: 6 mins
Preparation time: 10 mins

3½ cups (875 ml) water
24 ready-made fishballs (see note)
1 fish or *ikan bilis* stock cube
½ tablespoon soy sauce
2 tablespoons preserved dried Chinese cabbage (*tang chai*)
1 teaspoon ground white pepper
75 g (3 oz) dried glass noodles (*tang hoon*), soaked in warm
   water until soft, about 5 minutes
2 green onions (scallions), chopped, to garnish
Sliced red finger-length chillies and soy sauce, to serve

1 Bring the water to a boil in a pot. Add the fishballs and simmer
gently for 3 minutes, then add the stock cube, soy sauce,
preserved Chinese cabbage and pepper. Simmer for 3 more
minutes.

2 Divide the glass noodles into 6 individual serving bowls and
top up with 4 fishballs. Pour in the hot soup. Garnish with the
chopped green onions and serve with sliced red chillies and soy
sauce on the side.

**Note: Fishballs are available in various forms in Japanese, Chinese
and Vietnamese or Thai specialty stores. They are precooked
and made of tapiocal flour and bits of fish. Look for them in the
refrigerated or frozen foods sections.**

Bak Kut Teh Pork Rib Soup

This robust soup is traditionally eaten as a breakfast dish with *yew char kway* (Chinese fried dough crullers) and a pot of Chinese tea on the side. *Bak kut teh* spice mixes are available in many Chinese grocery stores or supermarkets.

Serves 3–4   Cooking time: 1 hour 15 mins
Preparation time: 10 mins

600 g (1⅓ lbs) pork ribs, cut into pieces
150 g (5 oz) lean pork
1 sachet *bak kut teh* spices
10 cups (2.5 litres) water or pork stock
3 tablespoons soy sauce
1 teaspoon salt
1 teaspoon sugar
Chopped fresh coriander leaves (cilantro), to garnish
Yew char kway (Chinese crullers), to serve

1 Combine the pork ribs, lean pork, *bak kut te* spices sachet and water in a large pot. Bring to a boil over medium heat, reduce the heat to low and simmer, covered, for 30 minutes.

2 Add the soy sauce, salt and sugar. Simmer for another 45 minutes, or until the pork is fork tender.

3 Remove the lean pork and shred into small pieces. Strain the stock into individaul serving bowls and divide the lean pork and pork ribs between them. Garnish with chopped fresh coriander leaves and serve with the *yew char kway* on the side.

Note: Every hawker stall puts a different spin on this dish. Some season it with dark soy sauce, others with regular soy sauce; use whichever you prefer. You can make your own spice bag with 1 cinnamon stick, 4–5 cloves, 1 pod star anise, 1 teaspoon black peppercorns and 1 tablespoon Chinese wolfberries (*kei chee*). Tie these in a piece of muslin cloth.

Sop Kambing Spiced Mutton Soup

This fragrant mutton soup is always served with crusty baguette on the side. Lamb, which makes a milder-flavoured soup, can be used instead of mutton. If lamb is used, the cooking time should be reduced slightly.

Serves 3–4 Cooking time: 1 hour
Preparation time: 15 mins plus 1 hour marinating time

7 tablespoons oil
10 Asian shallots, sliced
400 g (14 oz) boneless lamb or mutton, cut into shreds
6½ cups (1.5 litres) lamb or chicken stock or water
1 cinnamon stick
½ pod star anise
4 cardamom pods
1 teaspoon salt
1 teaspoon ground black pepper
Large handful fresh coriander leaves (cilantro), to garnish
Baguette slices, to serve

Spice Paste
5 Asian shallots
4 cloves garlic
4 slices fresh ginger root
6 mm (½ in) fresh turmeric root, sliced
1 teaspoon ground cumin
1 teaspoon ground fennel
2 tablespoons ground coriander

1 Heat the oil in a wok over medium-low heat. Stir-fry the sliced shallots, stirring, until crisp and golden brown, 4–6 minutes. Drain on paper towels and set aside. (You can save the oil for use as a condiment.)

2 Grind the Spice Paste ingredients until very fine and mix with the lamb. Set aside to marinate at room temperature, covered, for 1 hour.

3 Bring the stock or water to a boil in a large pot. Add the cinnamon, star anise, cardamoms, lamb with all its marinade, salt and pepper. Return to a boil and let it bubble vigorously for 15 minutes, then reduce the heat, cover the pot and simmer gently for 40 minutes. Serve garnished with coriander leaves and chunks of French baguette.

Soto Ayam Chicken Soup

One of our "cold-weather" favourites, this fragrant chicken soup is served with a spicy sauce on the side.

Serves 4–6 Cooking time: 50 mins
Preparation time: 25 mins plus 10 mins standing time

4 tablespoons oil
5 cups (1.25 litres) water or chicken stock
1 whole chicken, cleaned
1 teaspoon salt
90 g (3 oz) dried glass noodles (*tang hoon*), soaked in lukewarm water for 10 minutes to soften
2 potatoes, boiled, peeled and diced
Fresh coriander leaves (cilantro) or Chinese celery leaves, to garnish

Spices
6 candlenuts or macadamia nuts
1 teaspoon black peppercorns
10 Asian shallots
5 cloves garlic
1 thumb-sized piece fresh turmeric root
4 slices fresh ginger root
2 stalks lemongrass, tender inner part of bottom third only

Sauce
6 bird's-eye chillies, pounded to a coarse paste
2 tablespoons dark soy sauce
2 tablespoons fresh lime juice
1 teaspoon sugar

1 To prepare the Spices, grind the candlenuts and peppercorns together to a coarse powder. Add the remaining spices and grind until very fine. Heat the oil in a wok over medium heat and stir-fry all the Spices ingredients for 4 minutes, until fragrant.

2 Add the water or stock, chicken and salt. Simmer, partially covered, for 35 minutes, then turn off the heat.

3 Let the chicken sit in the hot stock for 10 minutes, then remove from the stock and transfer to a clean work surface. Remove and discard the skin. Pull the meat off the bones and shred into small strips. Return the bones to the stock and simmer, covered, for another 10 minutes.

4 Divide the dried glass noodles, chicken meat and diced potatoes into individual serving bowls. Strain the stock and ladle it into the bowls over the chicken and noodles, then garnish each bowl with the coriander leaves.

5 Combine all the Sauce ingredients in a dipping bowl and serve on the side.

Note: To turn this soup into a complete meal, add a handful of blanched fresh yellow noodles and bean sprouts to each bowl. Or you can eat it with rice.

Duck and Salted Vegetable Soup

An unlikely blend of flavours, you might think, but the tangy, meaty, aromatic result is immensely comforting on a cold day.

Serves 4–6 Cooking time: 1½ hours
Preparation time: 10 mins

1 duck, cleaned and cut into 8 pieces
200 g (7 oz) pork leg, cut into chunks
6½ cups (1.5 litres) water
400 g (14 oz) salted pickled mustard vegetable
  (*kiam chye*)
4 preserved sour plums
3 tomatoes, quartered
1 teaspoon sugar
4 green finger-length chillies
2 tablespoons brandy or cognac

1 Trim off any excess fat from the duck and place in a large pot with the pork leg and water. Bring to a boil and cook for 1¼ hours or until the meat are very tender.

2 Slice the salted vegetable into large pieces and add to the pot with the sour plums, tomatoes and sugar. Simmer, covered, for 10 minutes more. Skim off the oil from the surface of the soup.

3 Break the green chillies into small pieces with your fingers and stir them into the soup with the brandy. Serve hot with rice.

Bakwan Kepiting Soup

"*Bakwan*" means meatball for Hokkien and "*kepiting*" is Malay for crab. If you don't live near a good seafood market, canned crabmeat can be used. In his university days, Chris made this soup with canned crabmeat to great success (and accolades by fellow students).

Serves 6   Cooking time: 15 mins
Preparation time: 20 mins

4.5 kg (10 lbs) small fresh crabs in their
  shells, washed
3 tablespoons oil
6 cloves garlic, chopped
75 g (½ cup) finely sliced fresh or
  canned bamboo shoots
250 g (1¼ cups) ground pork
2 tablespoons finely chopped fresh
  coriander leaves (cilantro)
1 teaspoon salt
½ teaspoon ground white pepper
2 tablespoons soy sauce
6½ cups (1.5 litres) water or
  light pork stock

1 Bring a large pot of water to a boil over high heat, add the crabs, return to a boil and simmer for 6 minutes. Drain the crabs and when cool, remove all the meat and roe (if any), discarding the lungs and fibrous tissue. Reserve the body shells.

2 Heat the oil over medium heat and stir-fry the garlic until light brown, 2–3 minutes. Mix half the garlic and its oil, crabmeat, crab roe, half the bamboo shoots, ground pork, coriander leaves, salt, pepper and half the soy sauce together.

3 Stuff each crab shell with the crabmeat mixture. Shape the remaining stuffing into small balls. Bring the water or stock to a boil and slip in the stuffed shells and crabmeat balls. Simmer for 5–6 minutes or until cooked through. Stir in the remaining bamboo shoots, garlic and soy sauce. Serve hot, garnished with fresh coriander leaves.

Rojak Mixed Salad with Sweet Spicy Dressing

Is it Chinese? Is it Malay? Whichever, this is a true off-spring of the Singapore soil, once sold only by street hawkers. A spicy salad with all the flavours of the tropics, and a production number that should be stirred up in front of your adoring guests! Don't let it sit around, as it waters out after a while.

Serves 4–5 Cooking time: 7 mins
Preparation time: 20 mins

150 g (5 oz) *kangkong* (water spinach)
125 g (2½ cups) fresh bean sprouts, washed and drained
2 *yew char kway* (Chinese fried dough crullers)
4 deep-fried tofu squares (*tau pok*)
150 g (5 oz) fresh pineapple, sliced
200 g (7 oz) *bangkwang* (yambean or jicama), peeled and sliced
1 cucumber
4 tablespoons coarsely ground peanuts
1 small wild ginger bud (*bunga kantan*), shredded

Dressing
1 tablespoon tamarind pulp
⅔ cup (150 ml) water
1 generous tablespoon dried prawn paste (*belachan*)
4 red finger-length chillies, deseeded and finely chopped
1 tablespoon sugar
3 tablespoons *hay koh* (black prawn sauce)
3 teaspoons fresh lime juice

1 Trim and discard 2.5 cm (1 in) from the root ends of the *kangkong* and wash well. Bring a large pot of water to a rolling boil. Blanch the bean sprouts for 30 seconds, then remove and drain. Blanch the *kangkong* for 1 minute or until just tender and drain. Chop the *kangkong* into 5-cm (2-in) lengths. Toast the crullers and deep-fried tofu hot in a toaster oven or broiler grill until they are crisp on the outside, 4–5 minutes, turning frequently.

2 To make the Dressing, mash the tamarind pulp in the water. Strain to obtain the juice, discarding the solids. Roast the dried prawn paste over an open flame until blackened and fragrant. Grind the chillies, *hay koh* and sugar until fine and transfer to a large mixing bowl.

3 Stir the dried prawn paste into the chilli mixture until smooth. Slowly stir in the lime juice and ⅔ of the tamarind juice. Taste it: it should be hot, sweet, sharp and smoky. Add more sugar, tamarind juice, or lime juice if necessary.

4 Add the bean sprouts and *kangkong* to the bowl. With a sharp knife, slice in the pineapple, *bangkwang* and cucumber in bite-sized chunks. Toss well. Snip in the deep-fried tofu and crullers with sharp scissors. Sprinkle in most of the ground peanuts and toss again. Serve sprinkled with more ground peanuts and shredded ginger bud.

Breads, Rice and Noodles

Roti John Fried Bread with Mutton and Egg

A throwback to colonial days, this recipe is endowed with an Anglo-Saxon name in honour of the foreign bread it's made with! Made at home, this is much less oily and more healthy than the hawker version.

Serves 4–5 Preparation time: 15 mins plus 1 hour marinating time
Cooking time: 20 mins

250 g (1¼ cups) ground lamb or mutton
1 small onion, chopped
2 cloves garlic, finely minced
4 tablespoons chopped fresh coriander leaves
  (cilantro)
½ teaspoon ground cloves
¾ teaspoon ground cinnamon
½ teaspoon ground nutmeg
¾ teaspoon ground black pepper
1 teaspoon salt
1 medium baguette-type loaf (such as a bâtard)
5 eggs
2 tablespoons oil
Bottled sweet chilli sauce, sliced tomato and
  cucumber, to serve

1 Mix the lamb with the onion, garlic, coriander leaves, clove, cinnamon, nutmeg, black pepper and salt. Refrigerate for 1 hour. Cut the bread loaf into half horizontally, then cut each half into 3 or 4 pieces. Set aside, uncovered, to dry out slightly.

2 Beat 2 of the eggs and set aside. Crack the remaining 3 eggs into the meat mixture and mix loosely—it should be sloppy and uneven in texture.

3 Lightly grease a large skillet with a little of the oil and set over medium-low heat. Brush the cut sides of a piece of bread with some of the beaten egg, then coat the bread with a layer of the meat mixture, pressing it gently into the bread to form a smooth coating. Place it in the pan, face down, and fry for 8–10 minutes, turning after 5 minutes, so the meat is browned and the bread is crisp. Repeat with the remaining bread and meat mixture. Do not crowd the pan; fry in 2 or 3 batches.

4 Serve hot with the bottled sweet chilli sauce, tomato and cucumber on the side.

Roti Prata Crispy Pan-Fried Bread

Whereas the true Indian *paratha* is made with whole-wheat flour, this multilayered pan-fried bread, also known as *roti channai* in Malaysia, is made with white flour. Hawkers flip the dough, whirling it through the air until it is tissue-thin. For the novice it is easier to stretch it rather like strudel dough, as we've described here.

Makes about 12–14 prata
Cooking time: 4 mins per prata
Preparation time: 40 mins plus 45 mins standing time

500 g (3¼ cups) plain flour, sifted
1 teaspoon salt
1 teaspoon sugar
½ cup (125 ml) lukewarm water
4 tablespoons lukewarm milk
⅔ cup (165 ml) oil
Vegetable or meat curry gravy, to serve

1 Combine the flour, salt and sugar in a mixing bowl. Mix in the water, milk and 2 tablespoons of the oil with your hands and knead gently but constantly for about 7 minutes, adding more water or flour as necessary for a soft, coherent dough. Pinch off pieces the size of large plums and shape into balls. Roll the balls in the remaining oil to coat and place on a plate. Cover with plastic wrap and let stand for 45 minutes.

2 Heat a skillet, preferably non-stick, over medium-high heat.

3 Lightly grease a clean work surface. Place a dough ball on it and dab with a bit more oil. Flatten the dough lightly with your fingers, then stretch it outwards, working from the centre all the way to the edge and moving clockwise or anticlockwise around the circle. Try to make the dough as thin and even as you can.

4 Fold two opposite edges into the centre and then fold the other two edges to the centre on top of the first two, to make a rough square. Drop the prata onto the pan, folded sides downwards, and fry for 2–3 minutes or until the underside is browned. Flip the prata and brown the other side, 2 more minutes. Transfer to a plate. Repeat with the remaining dough balls.

5 Just before serving, stack the prata and clap them very quickly between your hands so they crumple up. They will spring back into shape, but their internal layers will now be fluffed up. Serve with plenty of hot curry gravy on the side.

Note: To make an egg-filled prata, crack an egg onto the stretched dough and smear it around a bit before folding and frying it. Large pratas folded around ground meat, onion and egg before frying are called *murtabaks*.

Prawn Fried Rice

This is a basic fried rice that you can embellish with vegetables, herbs and anything else you like.

Serves 2 Cooking time: 7 mins
Preparation time: 5 mins

1 tablespoon oil
3 cloves garlic, minced
2 eggs
150 g (5 oz) fresh prawns, peeled
250 g (2½ cups) cold cooked rice
1 tablespoon soy sauce
½ teaspoon ground black pepper
½ teaspoon salt
Pickled Green Chillies (page 25), to serve

1 Heat the oil in a wok over high heat and stir-fry the garlic for 1 minute, until lightly browned. Crack in the eggs and stir for a few seconds until they are almost set, then chop them roughly with the edge of the wok ladle.

2 Add the prawns and toss for 2 minutes, then add all the remaining ingredients and fry for about 3 minutes more until the rice is heated through and the prawns are fully cooked. Serve hot with Pickled Green Chillies on the side.

Quick Rice with Chicken

With the assistance of a microwave, this delicious, wholesome meal can easily be made on a busy weekday evening.

Serves 2 Cooking time: 20 mins
Preparation time: 10 mins

200 g (1 cup) uncooked rice
330 ml (1½ cups) water
200 g (1 cup) skinless chicken thigh or breast, cut into cubes
2 tablespoons oyster sauce
1 tablespoon dark soy sauce
½ teaspoon sugar
1 teaspoon ground white or black pepper
4 thin slices fresh ginger root
Chopped green onions (scallions) and sliced red chillies, to garnish

1 Wash the rice well, drain and combine with the water in a microwave-safe bowl with a cover. Cover and microwave for 8 minutes on high.

2 While the rice is cooking, mix the chicken cubes with the oyster sauce, soy sauce, sugar, pepper and ginger.

3 Stir the chicken mixture into the rice, cover and microwave for another 9–10 minutes on high. Let the rice stand for 3 minutes before serving, garnished with chopped green onions and sliced red chillies.

Malay-Style Nasi Goreng Fried Rice

This is a spicy Malay version of basic fried rice. Add colour and crunch with diced vegetables of your choice.

Serves 2–3 Cooking time: 8 mins
Preparation time: 15 mins

4 tablespoons oil
500 g (5 cups) cold cooked rice
200 g (1 cup) cooked shredded chicken
¾ teaspoon salt
3 eggs
Sliced cucumber and Fried Chilli Sambal (page 28), to serve

Spice Paste
2–3 red finger-length chillies, deseeded
8 Asian shallots
4 cloves garlic
1 tablespoon dried prawn paste (belachan), dry-roasted
1 tablespoon dried prawns, soaked until soft

1 Grind all the Spice Paste ingredients together until fine.

2 Heat the oil in a wok over medium-high heat and stir-fry the Spice Paste for 4–5 minutes until fragrant. Add the cold cooked rice, shredded chicken and salt and toss well for 1–2 minutes to coat the rice grains evenly with the Spice Paste and heat them through.

3 Push the rice to the sides of the wok to make a well in the centre and crack the eggs into it. Scramble until softly set, then combine with the rice to mix. Serve with sliced cucumber and Fried Chilli Sambal on the side.

Hainanese Chicken Rice

You know a dish deserves ambassadorial status when it appears on a Singapore Airlines menu. Originating from Hainan Island, this dish was originally made using a special breed of chicken with yellow fat and particularly flavourful flesh, from Wenchang province. The chilli sauce is a purely Singaporean invention.

Serves 4–6   Cooking time: 45 mins
Preparation time: 30 mins

1 large chicken
10 cups (2.5 litres) water
3 cloves garlic, peeled
2 slices fresh ginger root
Sesame oil, for rubbing Thick dark
   soy sauce, fresh sprigs of coriander
   leaves (cilantro), cucumber slices,
   crispy fried shallots, to serve

Rice
600 g (3 cups) uncooked rice
2 tablespoons finely chopped garlic
1½ tablespoons finely chopped fresh
   ginger root
1 tablespoon finely chopped shallots
2 pandanus leaves, tied into a knot
2 teaspoons salt, or to taste

Chilli Sauce
6 red finger-length chillies
3–5 bird's-eye chillies
2 cloves garlic
2 teaspoons minced fresh ginger root
½ teaspoon sugar
½ teaspoon salt, or to taste
2 tablespoons fresh lime juice

Ginger Sauce
100 g (½ cup) peeled and sliced fresh
   old ginger root
1 tablespoon oil

1 Clean the chicken thoroughly. Remove the excess fat and reserve. Bring the water to a rolling boil in a large, deep pot. Fully submerge the chicken in the boiling water. Return to a rolling boil. Simmer vigorously, partially covered, for 15 minutes, then cover tightly, switch off the heat and let stand for 20 minutes.

2 Remove the chicken from the stock. Rub the chicken skin with the sesame oil and set aside.

3 To prepare the Rice, wash the rice grains well and drain, then spread out on a large plate and let it dry, 10–15 minutes.

4 Chop the reserved chicken fat into small pieces. Combine with 2 tablespoons cold water in a small pot and cook over low heat for 10–15 minutes, until the water has evaporated and the fat has rendered.

5 Heat 5 tablespoons of the rendered chicken fat in a wok over medium heat. Stir-fry the garlic, ginger and shallots for the Rice until fragrant, 1–2 minutes. Add the rice and stir-fry gently for 2–3 minutes or until the grains turn translucent. Transfer the rice to a rice cooker, add the pandanus leaves, salt and 750 ml (3 cups) of the stock from the chicken pot. Switch on the rice cooker and leave to cook.

6 Make the Chilli Sauce by blending all the ingredients to form a paste, then add 2 tablespoons of the chicken stock and blend until combined.

7 Make the Ginger Sauce by blending the ginger to a paste, then add the oil and 1 tablespoon of the chicken stock and blend until combined.

8 Chop the chicken into bite-sized pieces before serving with the cooked rice, sauces and garnishes. Serve any remaining chicken stock as soup.

Nasi Lemak Fragrant Coconut Rice

This soothingly rich rice dish is meant to be accompanied by several side dishes and sambals of contrasting textures, including sliced cucumber, Fried Chilli Sambal (page 28), Crispy Ikan Bilis with Peanuts (page 27), a fried egg and a small whole fish, rubbed with salt and deep-fried to a crisp. To make this a heartier meal, serve it with fried chicken wings or drumsticks, a sambal vegetable and perhaps some achar pickles on the side.

Serves 3–4 Cooking time: 30 mins
Preparation time: 10 mins plus 30 mins standing time

300 g (1½ cups) uncooked rice
1 cup (250 ml) thick coconut milk
1 cup (250 ml) water
2 pandanus leaves, tied into a knot
1½ teaspoons salt

1 Wash the rice well until the water runs virtually clear. Drain well. Combine the rice, coconut milk, water and pandanus leaves in a rice cooker and mix well. Set aside to soak for 30 minutes.

2 Stir in the salt and switch the rice cooker on. When done, fluff with a fork and serve hot.

3 Alternatively, bring the rice to a boil in a heavy-based pot (coconut milk scorches easily), then reduce the heat to very low and cook, tightly covered, 20–25 minutes or until done.

Note: The more recently the rice has been harvested, the less water it needs to cook. When cooking rice, it is better to err on the side of caution with the liquid—you can always add a little bit more water as the rice cooks, but you can do little to revive soggy rice.

Mee Goreng Spicy Egg Noodles

A spicy twist on stir-fried Chinese noodles, this is one of the very few noodle dishes found in Singapore Indian cooking.

Serves 3–4   Cooking time: 7 mins
Preparation time: 15 mins

3 tablespoons oil
2 cloves garlic, crushed
150 g (5 oz) fresh prawns, peeled
500 g (1 lb) fresh yellow wheat noodles *(mee)* or 250 g
   (8 oz) dried thick egg noodles, boiled and drained
75 g (1½ cups) fresh bean sprouts
100 g (2 cups) *choy sum* (Chinese greens) or bok choy,
   separated into individual leaves
3 tablespoons water
4 tablespoons Fried Chilli Sambal (page 28)
1 potato, boiled, peeled and diced
2 tomatoes, quartered
1 teaspoon salt, or to taste
3 eggs

1 Heat the oil in a wok over high heat and stir-fry the garlic for 1 minute until golden and fragrant. Add the prawns, noodles, bean sprouts and greens, and fry for 2 minutes.

2 Add the water, Fried Chilli Sambal, potato, tomatoes and salt. Stir vigorously for 2 minutes. Push the noodles to the sides of the wok, crack the eggs into the centre and scramble until just set, 1–2 minutes. Combine well to mix. Serve hot.

Note: Instead of prawns, you can use shredded cooked chicken or mutton.

Beehoon Goreng Fried Rice Noodles

Like most Asian noodle dishes, this one is quick to prepare.
The secret ingredient is Western-style tomato ketchup.

Serves 2-3 Cooking time: 10 mins
Preparation time: 15 mins plus 15 mins standing time

150 g (5 oz) dried rice vermicelli *(beehoon)*
3 boneless chicken thighs, cut into small pieces
½ teaspoon ground cumin
½ teaspoon ground coriander
¼ teaspoon ground cinnamon
¼ teaspoon ground turmeric
4 cloves garlic, finely chopped
2–3 tablespoons bottled sweet chilli sauce
2–3 tablespoons tomato ketchup
1 tablespoon soy sauce
2 teaspoons sugar, or to taste
1 teaspoon salt, or to taste
4 tablespoons water
5 tablespoons oil
1 small onion, sliced
20 curry leaves
5 cabbage leaves, sliced
2–3 green finger-length chillies, deseeded and thickly sliced
3 eggs

1 Soak the dried rice vermicelli in cold water for 15 minutes until softened but not soggy. Drain well. Cut into 10-cm (4-in) lengths.

2 Mix the chicken with the spices and garlic. Let it marinate for 15 minutes. Mix the 3 sauces with the sugar and salt. Set aside.

3 Heat the oil in a wok over medium-high heat. Add the onion and stir-fry for 2 minutes, then add the curry leaves, cabbage, chillies and marinated chicken. Stir-fry for 3–4 minutes or until the chicken is just cooked through.

4 Add the rice vermicelli and stir for 1 minute, then add the sauce mixture and stir-fry vigorously for 2–3 minutes. Push the noodles to the sides of the wok, crack the eggs into the centre and scramble until just set. Stir to mix well and serve immediately.

Char Kway Teow Fried Rice Stick Noodles

This is one of those dishes that inspire fanatical allegiance to a stall that gets it right. What made it memorable in days of yore was generous amounts of pork lard and cracklings (*chee yow char*) and fat blood cockles (*see hum*). These days, health-conscious diners eschew one or both of these, and in recent years we've seen new versions of Char Kway Teow topped with mounds of steamed greens and crispy whitebait (smelt).

Serves 3–4   Cooking time: 5 mins
Preparation time: 15 mins

4 tablespoons lard or cooking oil
1½ tablespoons crushed garlic
1 dried sweet Chinese sausage *(lap cheong)*, very thinly sliced
1 fish cake (150 g/5 oz), thinly sliced
1 small squid, cleaned, head discarded, body sliced into rings
150 g (5 oz) fresh prawns, peeled
350 g (12 oz) fresh flat rice noodles *(kway teow)* or 200 g (7 oz) dried *hor fun* rice stick noodles, soaked in water until soft, then drained
75 g (1½ cups) fresh bean sprouts
3 eggs
3 tablespoons *kecap manis* (thick black sweet soy sauce)
1 teaspoon soy sauce
1–2 tablespoons chilli sauce
3 tablespoons water

1 Heat the lard or oil in a wok over high heat and stir-fry the garlic for 1 minute, until golden and fragrant. Add the dried sweet Chinese sausage, fish cake, squid and prawns and stir-fry for 2 minutes.

2 Add the bean sprouts, *kway teow*, soy sauces, chilli sauce and water. Stir vigorously for 3–4 minutes until well mixed. Noodles should be moist and aromatic. Add a little water if needed. Taste and adjust the seasonings and serve hot.

Note: If you can get fresh shelled blood cockles, then add them half-way through step 2. They should be just barely cooked when the noodles are ready. If you cannot get thick black sweet soy sauce, substitute 2 tablespoons thick dark soy sauce or normal dark soy sauce mixed with 1 tablespoon brown sugar.

Fried Hokkien Mee

Modern foodcourt versions of this dish are all too often terribly sloppy in execution and texture. The old-fashioned version, after which this is patterned, was moist and highly fragrant and, if packed to take home, was (and is still, occasionally) wrapped up in a large dried "opair" leaf, which added an ineffable kick to the aroma.

Serves 3–4   Cooking time: 30 mins
Preparation time: 20 mins

2½ cups (625 ml) water
500 g (1 lb) belly pork
4 tablespoons oil
2 tablespoons crushed garlic
300 g (10 oz) fresh yellow wheat noodles *(mee)* or 150 g (5 oz)
   dried thick egg noodles, soaked in warm water for 30 minutes, drained
125 g (4 oz) dried rice vermicelli *(beehoon)*, soaked in warm water for 10
   minutes, drained
250 g (8 oz) fresh prawns, peeled
1 piece fish cake, sliced
1 small squid, cleaned, discarded, body sliced into rings
80 g (2 cups) Chinese chives *(koo chai)*, cut into short lengths
75 g (1½ cups) fresh bean sprouts
2 tablespoons fish sauce
¾ teaspoon ground white pepper
¼ teaspoon sugar
4 eggs
Sambal Belachan with Kaffir Lime Leaf (page 26) or Fried Chilli Sambal
   (page 28), sliced red chilli and cut kalamansi limes, to serve

1 Bring the water to a boil in a large pot over medium heat. Add the belly pork and simmer gently for 20 minutes. Let the pork sit in the stock for 10 minutes, then remove and slice into thin strips. Measure out 1 cup (250 ml) of the stock and set aside.

2 Heat the oil in a wok over very high heat. Stir-fry the crushed garlic for 30 seconds until light brown and fragrant, then add both types of noodles and stir-fry vigorously for 1–2 minutes or until the noodles are dry and browned but not burnt.

3 Add the reserved stock—which the noodles should soak up rapidly—prawns, fish cake, squid, Chinese chives, bean sprouts, fish sauce, pepper and sugar. Stir-fry very vigorously for 3–4 minutes over high heat. Crack in the eggs and stir well. They should set quickly. The noodles are done when they are cooked through and moist but not soggy—add more stock if necessary—and seafood is fully cooked. Serve with the accompaniments.

Beef Hor Fun Rice Noodles

This is a hearty and filling dish. Chris likes to mix the leftover noodles with a beaten egg and fry them slowly until crusty in a non-stick pan for breakfast.

Serves 3–4   Cooking time: 6 mins
Preparation time: 15 mins plus 30 mins marinating time

250 g (8 oz) tender sirloin beef
2 tablespoons rice wine
1½ tablespoons finely minced fresh ginger root
1 teaspoon ground black pepper
2 tablespoons oyster sauce
2 tablespoons sesame oil
2 teaspoons cornstarch
4 tablespoons oil
500 g (1 lb) fresh flat rice noodles *(hor fun)* or *kway teow*
    or 250 g (8 oz) dried rice stick noodles, soaked in water
    for 15 minutes until soft, then drained
2 tablespoons dark soy sauce
⅔ cup (150 ml) water
3 green onions (scallions), sliced into short lengths
Pickled Green Chillies (page 25), to serve

1 Slice the beef into thin strips. Mix with the rice wine, ginger, pepper, oyster sauce and sesame oil. Set aside to marinate, covered and refrigerated, for at least 20 minutes and up to 3 hours. When ready to cook, mix the cornstarch into the beef.

2 Heat 3 tablespoons of the oil in a wok over high heat until smoking and quickly stir-fry the noodles with the dark soy sauce for 2 minutes, tossing vigorously, until slightly browned. Remove from the wok.

3 Add the remaining oil to the wok and fry the beef for 2 minutes. Add the water and return the noodles to the wok. Fry for 1 more minute, then add the green onions and toss well for 30 seconds to wilt them. Serve immediately with Pickled Green Chillies on the side.

Note: *Hor fun* noodles are broader than *kway teow*. If you cannot find the former, use the widest *kway teow* you can find.

Laksa Rice Noodle Soup

Different versions of noodles in spicy broths, sometimes containing coconut, sometimes not, can be found across the length and breadth of the Malay Peninsula. Though not traditional for this dish, Chris likes to squeeze fresh lime juice over the sambal to cut the richness of the gravy.

Serves 4–6 Cooking time: 16 mins
Preparation time: 20 mins

4 tablespoons dried prawns, soaked until soft
6 tablespoons oil
6½ cups (1.5 litres) thin coconut milk
1 teaspoon salt
2 teaspoons sugar
600 g (1⅓ lbs) fresh *laksa* noodles or 250 g (8 oz) dried thin spaghetti, cooked and drained
100 g (2 cups) fresh bean sprouts
16 fresh large prawns
150 g (5 oz) blood cockles (optional)
Finely sliced *laksa* leaves *(daun kesom* or Vietnamese mint), and Fried Chilli Sambal (page 28), to serve

Spice Paste
2 small onions, sliced
6 cloves garlic
8–12 dried red finger-length chillies, soaked until soft
3 stalks lemongrass, tender bottom third portion only, sliced
5 slices galangal root
1 tablespoon dried prawn paste *(belachan)*, dry-roasted
1 thumb-sized piece fresh turmeric root, peeled

1 Grind all the Spice Paste ingredients together until fine. Set aside

2 Grind the dried prawns until fine and set aside. Heat the oil in a wok over medium heat and stir-fry the Spice Paste for 6–8 minutes, until thick and fragrant. Add the coconut milk, bring to a boil and add the salt, sugar and ground dried prawns. Simmer uncovered for 5 minutes and adjust the taste with salt or sugar as necessary.

3 Blanch the noodles and bean sprouts separately in boiling water for 30 seconds. Blanch the prawns in fresh boiling water for 2 minutes or until cooked through, then drain, shell and slice in half lengthwise. Blanch the cockles, if using, in boiling water for 1 minute. Discard any unopened cockles and shuck the cooked ones.

4 To serve, divide the bean sprouts and noodles into individual serving bowls and garnish with the sliced prawns and cockles. Ladle the hot coconut gravy over each portion of noodles and let diners help themselves to the *laksa* leaves and sambal.

Nasi Ulam Herbal Rice Salad

The Peranakans of Kelantan, Malaysia, are known for their variations on this cold rice salad, which may contain up to fifteen different herbs, including the quirkily-named *daun kentut* or flatulence leaf.

Serves 4–5   Cooking time: 25 mins
Preparation time: 30 mins

2 whole *ikan selar* (yellowstripe trevally), or other small fine-fleshed white fish, about 500 g (1 lb) total
6 tablespoons oil
6 Asian shallots, thinly sliced
4 cloves garlic, thinly sliced
200 g (2 cups) freshly grated coconut
4 runner beans or 10–12 string beans
½ cucumber, peeled and deseeded
2 stalks lemongrass, tender inner part of bottom third only
4 kaffir lime leaves *(daun limau purut)*
Small handful Asian basil leaves *(daun kemangi* or *daun selaseh)*
Small handful laksa leaves *(daun kesom* or Vietnamese mint)
Small handful mint leaves
1 turmeric leaf *(daun kunyit)*
1 teaspoon salt
500 g (5 cups) cold cooked rice
Sambal Belachan with Kaffir Lime Leaf (page 26), to serve

1 Clean the fish and pat dry. Grill under a hot broiler grill for 10 minutes, turning once. Let cool completely, then skin and debone. Flake the flesh finely and set aside.

2 Heat the oil in a wok over medium heat and stir-fry the sliced shallots and garlic until light brown, 3–4 minutes. Drain on paper towels.

3 In a clean wok or skillet over low heat, dry-fry the grated coconut for 6–8 minutes, stirring constantly, until golden brown.

4 Slice the beans very thinly and finely dice the cucumber. Slice the lemongrass as thinly as you can with a very sharp knife. Shred all the herbs finely into fine threads.

5 Toss all the ingredients together with the rice until thoroughly mixed. Serve immediately with Sambal Belachan with Kaffir Lime Leaf on the side.

Chicken and Duck

Braised Chicken Wings with Tofu and Kangkong

Sometimes referred to as *lo kai yik*, this very traditional recipe is not often seen outside the home nowadays. Serve it with hot rice and a red chilli, garlic and vinegar dip.

Serves 4–6 Cooking time: 30 mins
Preparation time: 15 mins

150 g (5 oz) *kangkong* (water spinach)
2 firm tofu cakes (*tau kwa*)
3 tablespoons oil
1½ tablespoons chopped garlic
1½ tablespoons chopped fresh ginger root
2 cubes fermented red tofu (*lam yee*)
1 tablespoon hoisin sauce
2 tablespoons oyster sauce
12 chicken wings, each cut into 3 joints
3 cups (750 ml) water

1 Trim and discard the root ends of the *kangkong*. Blanch the *kangkong* in boiling water for 2 minutes, then drain well. Cut each tofu square into 8 triangles.

2 Heat the oil in a wok over medium heat and stir-fry the garlic and ginger for 2 minutes. Add the fermented tofu and mash well with the wok spatula, then stir in the hoisin sauce, oyster sauce, chicken wings and water. Simmer uncovered for 20 minutes.

3 Add the *kangkong* and tofu and simmer for 5 more minutes. Dish up and serve immediately.

Opor Ayam Fragrant Coconut Chicken

This is our rendition of an Indonesian coconut curry.
It is slightly more complex than the original.

Serves 4–5   Preparation time: 15 mins
Cooking time: 45 mins

4 tablespoons oil
3 cups (700 ml) thin coconut milk
1 chicken, cut into 12 pieces
3 dried red finger-length chillies, soaked until soft, left whole
2 stalks lemongrass, tender inner part of bottom third only, bruised
4 kaffir lime leaves
1 teaspoon salt
1 teaspoon sugar

Spice Paste
3 slices galangal root
3 slices fresh ginger root
5 candlenuts or macadamia nuts
12 small shallots
1 thumb-size piece fresh turmeric root
3 cloves garlic
1 tablespoon ground coriander
1 teaspoon ground cumin
½ teaspoon ground black pepper

1 Grind all the Spice Paste ingredients into a thick, fine paste.

2 Heat the oil in a wok over medium heat and stir-fry the Spice Paste for 6 minutes, until thick and fragrant. Add 2 tablespoons of the coconut milk and stir-fry for 2 more minutes. Add the chicken pieces, chillies, lemongrass, kaffir lime leaves and remaining coconut milk. Simmer for 25 minutes.

3 Add the salt and sugar, increase the heat slightly and cook for 10 more minutes to thicken the gravy slightly. Serve hot.

Note: If you prefer the curry paler, leave out the turmeric. Grind the chillies with the Spice Paste if you want more heat. Chris prefers it subtle so he leaves them whole.

Ayam Tempra Sweet Soy Chicken

A recipe with hazy Portuguese origins, this stir-fry is given a spicy fillip with aromatics like lemongrass, garlic and kaffir lime leaves for a hot, sweet-and-sour flavour that is unique. This is Chris' take on a dish that has been in the family for decades.

Serves 2–3 Cooking time: 6 mins
Preparation time: 10 mins plus 15 mins marinating time

4 large boneless chicken thighs or 2 chicken breasts
½ teaspoon dried prawn paste (*belachan*), dry-roasted
1 tablespoon shaved palm sugar or dark brown sugar, finely chopped
1 tablespoon water
2 tablespoons *kecap manis* (thick black sweet soy sauce)
2 tablespoons oil
1 small onion, halved and thickly sliced
2 red finger-length chillies, sliced diagonally
3 cloves garlic, sliced
1 stalk lemongrass, tender inner part of bottom third only, thinly sliced diagonally
3 tablespoons fresh lime juice
⅓ teaspoon salt, or to taste

1 Cut the chicken into bite-sized chunks. Mash the dried prawn paste with the palm sugar, water and *kecap manis* until smooth and mix with the chicken. Set aside to marinate for 15 minutes at room temperature.

2 Heat the oil in a wok over high heat. Add the onion, chillies, garlic and lemongrass and stir-fry vigorously until softened and fragrant, 1–2 minutes. Add the chicken and stir-fry until it is just cooked through, 3–4 minutes more, then add the lime juice and salt and mix well. Serve hot with rice.

Chicken Wings in Dark Soy and Rice Wine

This dish is hearty and robust, very fragrant, and easily multiplied if you're cooking for a crowd.

Serves 3–4   Cooking time: 25 mins   Preparation time: 10 mins

8 chicken wings, each cut into 3 joints
⅓ cup (80 ml) rice wine
2 tablespoons sesame oil
1 teaspoon ground black pepper
8 dried black Chinese mushrooms, soaked until soft, hard stems removed, caps sliced in half
1 teaspoon salt
1 teaspoon sugar
2 tablespoons dark soy sauce
6 slices of fresh ginger root
2 cups (500 ml) water
2 green onions (scallions), cut into short lengths
1 tablespoon chopped celery leaves

1 Combine the chicken wings with the rice wine, sesame oil and black pepper. Let marinate for 1 hour, covered, at room temperature.

2 Combine the chicken wings, mushrooms and all the other ingredients, except the green onions and celery leaves, in a large pot. Bring to a boil over medium heat, partially cover and simmer for 20 minutes, or until the wings are tender. Increase the heat to reduce the sauce more during the last 5 minutes, if desired. Stir in the green onions and celery leaves and cook for 1 more minute. Serve piping hot.

Lemon Chicken

Though this dish has real elegance in its original Cantonese version, when prepared without care it can go horribly wrong (glutinous sauce, greasy chicken). We're happy to share with you a recipe for an unadulterated and truly delicious Lemon Chicken.

Serves 2–3   Cooking time: 10 mins   Preparation time: 15 mins

2 chicken breasts, skinned and deboned
1 egg, lightly beaten
4 tablespoons cornstarch
Oil, for deep-frying
Grated lemon zest, to garnish, if desired

Sauce
3 tablespoons lemon juice
2 tablespoons Chinese plum sauce
¾ cup (200 ml) water
2 teaspoons cornstarch
½ lemon, scrubbed, quartered and sliced paper thin

1 Combine all the Sauce ingredients in a bowl and set aside.

2 Lightly beat the chicken breasts to a thickness of 12 mm (½ in). Coat the chicken with the beaten egg and dredge in the cornstarch. Heat the oil in a wok over medium heat until shimmering and deep-fry the chicken until light golden brown, 5–7 minutes, turning once. Drain on paper towels and set aside.

3 Bring the Sauce to a boil over medium heat. Simmer for 2 more minutes until it thickens. Slice the chicken into serving pieces, pour the Sauce over. Serve immediately, garnished with the lemon zest.

Kari Ayam Spicy Chicken Curry

There are as many versions of this basic curry as there are spices in the pot. Serve with white rice or slice of baguette; Chris thinks toasted plain bagels are good with it too.

Serves 4–5 Cooking time: 55 mins Preparation time: 20 mins

1 large chicken, cut into 10–12 pieces
5 tablespoons oil
3 medium potatoes, peeled and quartered
3 cups (750 ml) thin coconut milk
1 teaspoon salt
1 teaspoon sugar

Spice Paste
1 small onion, sliced
3 slices fresh ginger root
4 cloves garlic
2 tablespoons ground coriander
1 tablespoon ground cumin
1 teaspoon ground fennel
2–3 teaspoons ground red pepper
1 teaspoon ground turmeric
½ teaspoon ground cinnamon
½ teaspoon ground cloves
½ teaspoon ground cardamom

1 Wash and pat dry the chicken. Remove and discard any excess fatty skin.

2 Grind all the Spice Paste ingredients together to form a paste, adding a little more water if necessary to keep the blades turning. Set aside.

3 Heat the oil in a wok over medium heat and fry the potatoes for 4–5 minutes until slightly browned. Remove with a slotted spoon and set aside. Add the Spice Paste to the wok and stir-fry for 6–7 minutes, stirring constantly, until fragrant.

4 Add the chicken pieces and stir well, then add the coconut milk, salt, sugar, potatoes and simmer, partially covered, for 40–45 minutes or until the chicken is tender. Serve hot.

Note: You can substitute 1 cinnamon stick, 4 cloves and 3 cardamom pods for their powdered form.

Ayam Kurmah Aromatic Chicken

This Malay interpretation of an Indian korma uses coconut milk instead of yoghurt or cream. Served with rice, this chicken dish is very addictive.

Serves 3–4 Preparation time: 15 mins plus 10 mins standing time
Cooking time: 1 hour

1¾ cups (400 ml) thin coconut milk
½ cup (125 ml) evaporated milk or cream
4 tablespoons raw almonds, ground
2 tablespoons fresh lime juice
3 tablespoons oil
1 small onion, sliced
2 teaspoons minced fresh ginger root, pounded to a paste
6 cardamom pods
6 cloves
2 stalks lemongrass, tender inner part of bottom third only, bruised
1 whole chicken, cut into 8–10 pieces
1¼ teaspoons salt
1¼ cups (300 ml) water
2 large potatoes, peeled and quartered
Crispy fried shallots, to garnish

Spice Paste
4 cloves garlic
6 candlenuts or macadamia nuts
2 tablespoons ground coriander
1½ tablespoons ground cumin
1 teaspoon ground fennel
1 teaspoon ground pepper
2 tablespoons water

1 Grind all the Spice Paste ingredients together to form a paste, adding a little more water, if necessary, to keep the baldes turning.

2 Mix the coconut milk, evaporated milk or cream, ground almonds and lime juice together. Set aside for 10 minutes so that it curdles slightly.

3 Heat the ghee or oil in a wok over medium heat. Stir-fry the onion for 3 minutes or until soft, then add the ginger, cardamoms, cloves, lemongrass and Spice Paste. Stir-fry for 5–6 minutes or until fragrant, stirring and scraping constantly to prevent scorching.

4 Add the coconut milk mixture, chicken, salt and water. Simmer for 30 minutes, then add the potatoes and simmer for another 20 minutes. Remove from the heat, garnish with the crispy fried shallots and serve.

Duck Braised in Dark Soy and Tamarind (Itek Sio)

Though simple to make, this dish does take time but is well worth the effort; the important thing is to cook the duck long and slowly until it is fork-tender and the sauce aromatic and glossy. It is traditionally sweetened with bruised lengths of sugar cane, but raw sugar gives the same flavour with less effort.

Serves 4–6 Cooking time: 3 hours
Preparation time: 10 mins plus 1 hour marinating time

1 whole duck, about 2.5 kg (5½ lbs)
1½ teaspoons salt
3 tablespoons ground coriander
2 teaspoons ground black pepper
2 tablespoons raw or brown sugar
4 tablespoons dark soy sauce
1 tablespoon tamarind pulp
¾ cup (180 ml) water
4 tablespoons oil
2 small onions, finely minced
12¾ cups (3 litres) water
2 cinnamon sticks
8 cloves
4 tablespoons chopped fresh coriander leaves
   (cilantro)

1 Clean the duck thoroughly and wipe dry. Mix the salt, coriander, pepper, sugar and soy sauce together and rub it all over the duck. Let marinate for 1 hour at room temperature.

2 Mash the tamarind pulp with the water. Strain to obtain the juice, discarding the solids. Set aside.

3 Heat the oil in a large wok over medium heat and stir-fry the onions until soft and light brown, 6–8 minutes. Put in the duck and fry, turning constantly, to brown the skin all over.

4 Add the tamarind juice, water, cinnamon and cloves. Bring to a gentle boil. Simmer, covered, for about 2½ hours or until the duck is very tender, turning the duck 2 or 3 times and topping up with more water if necessary. Transfer the duck to a clean chopping board and let it rest for 10 minutes. Meanwhile, turn the heat to high and reduce the sauce until thick and glossy.

5 Chop the duck into serving pieces. Arrange these on a serving plate, pour some sauce over them and sprinkle with chopped coriander leaves. Serve the extra sauce on the side.

Ayam Lemak Puteh Coconut Gravy Chicken

This pale, aromatic chicken dish is best served with biryani rice or yellow rice cooked with ground turmeric.

Serves 2–4   Preparation time: 20 mins   Cooking time: 50 mins

1 chicken, about 1.25 kg (2½ lbs)
1 teaspoon salt
4 tablespoons oil
2½ cups (625 ml) thin coconut milk
⅜ cup (100 ml) water
2 stalks lemongrass, tender inner part of bottom third only, bruised
1 tablespoon fish sauce
Juice of 1 lime

Spice Paste
1 small onion
3 cloves garlic
5 slices fresh galangal root
2 tablespoons ground coriander
1 tablespoon ground cumin
1 teaspoon ground fennel
½ teaspoon ground white pepper

1 Cut the chicken into 8 pieces and trim off any excess fat. Rub all over with the salt.

2 Grind all the Spice Paste ingredients together until very fine.

3 Heat the oil in a wok over medium heat and stir-fry the Spice Paste for 4 minutes, until thick and fragrant. Add 2 tablespoons of the coconut milk and stir-fry for 2 more minutes, stirring and scraping the wok constantly.

4 Add the remaining coconut milk, water, lemongrass and fish sauce. Bring to a boil. Add the chicken and simmer for 40–45 minutes or until the chicken is tender and cooked through. Drizzle with the lime juice and stir well before serving.

Sambal Roast Chicken

For the best flavour and texture the chicken is cooked twice—first simmered in a rich coconut milk gravy whose spices recall a satay marinade—and then grilled to crisp the skin. If you wish, you can cut the chicken into smaller individual serving pieces or use a couple of Cornish game hens.

Serves 4 Cooking time: 1 hour
Preparation time: 15 mins

4 tablespoons oil
1¾ cups (450 ml) coconut milk
6 kaffir lime leaves
2 stalks lemongrass, tender inner part of bottom third only, bruised
1 teaspoon salt
1 tablespoon shaved palm sugar or dark brown sugar
4 slices galangal root
1 fresh chicken, split in half

Spice Paste
½ small onion, sliced
3 slices fresh ginger root
3 cloves garlic
3–4 dried red finger-length chillies, soaked until soft
2 tablespoons ground coriander
1 tablespoon ground cumin
1 teaspoon ground fennel

1 Grind all the Spice Paste ingredients together until fine.

2 Heat the oil in a wok over medium heat and stir-fry the Spice Paste for 5 minutes until fragrant and thick. Add the coconut milk, kaffir lime leaves, lemongrass, salt, sugar and galangal. Stir well, then add the chicken and bring the contents to a boil. Simmer for 40 minutes, partially covered, turning the chicken a few times, until cooked through but not falling apart and the gravy is thick.

3 Remove the chicken from the gravy and transfer to a grill pan or broiler. Make several deep slashes in the thickest parts of the chicken and dribble the gravy liberally all over the chicken. Grill under high heat for 10–15 minutes, turning a few times and basting frequently with the gravy to build up a good crust, until browned all over. Serve with rice and the remaining gravy (reduce it a bit over high heat if desired) on the side.

Soy-Braised Chicken

This delicious dish is Cantonese in origin. Leftover sauce can be used to braise another chicken, or in fact any meat.

Serves 4–5 Cooking time: 1 hour
Preparation time: 10 mins

3 tablespoons oil
3 tablespoons sugar
1 whole chicken, excess fat removed
6½ cups (1.5 litres) water
5 tablespoons thick dark soy sauce
Large walnut-sized knob of galangal
    root, bruised
¾ teaspoon five spice powder
1 teaspoon salt
Sliced cucumber and sliced green
    onions (scallions), to serve
3 tablespoons sesame oil

1 Heat the oil and sugar together in a wok over medium heat, stirring frequently. Watch it like a hawk; when the sugar has melted and caramelised into little brown globules, add the chicken and roll it around in the caramel to coat.

2 Add the water, soy sauce, galangal, five spice powder and salt. Bring to a boil. Reduce the heat to low and simmer gently, covered, for 45–50 minutes, turning the chicken once, or until the chicken is tender but not falling apart. Turn off the heat and let the chicken sit in the hot liquid, covered, for another 10 minutes.

3 Gently lift out the chicken. Transfer to a chopping board and slice into small pieces. Pull any stray bits of meat off the bones, heap them in the centre of a serving platter, then surround with the chicken pieces. Garnish with cucumber and green onions.

4 Add the sesame oil to the sauce and reduce over high heat until slightly thickened, 6–8 minutes. Drizzle a little sauce over the chicken and serve any extra on the side.

Note: You can braise a duck in the same manner; use 10 cups (2.5 litres) of water and simmer the duck for 2 hours.

Seafood

Singapore Chilli Crab

One of our unofficial national dishes, chilli crab was once served up by stalls on the banks of the Kallang River as well as in seaside restaurants all around the island. Today the dish has several different incarnations. The gravy may be sweet, tart and ketchupy or slick with chilli oil. It may be thickened with beaten eggs, flavoured and textured with onions and chopped peanuts, or even made tangy with orange juice and pineapple. One thing is constant—the crabs (usually Sri Lankan green crabs) must be meaty and impeccably fresh.

Serves 2–4 Cooking time: 10 mins
Preparation time: 20 mins

5 kg (11 lbs) fresh crabs
5 tablespoons oil
2 small onions, sliced
8 cloves garlic, finely minced
2 tablespoons minced fresh ginger root
5–6 tablespoons bottled hot chilli sauce, such as Thai sriracha sauce
4 tablespoons tomato ketchup
1 teaspoon salt
1 teaspoon sugar
1½ cups (375 ml) water
Baguette slices, to serve

1 Remove the body shell of the crabs and discard the lungs and fibrous tissue. Cut the main body in half down the centre with a sharp cleaver, then cut each half into two pieces. Separate the claws from the body and crack them lightly with a mallet.

2 Heat the oil in a wok over high heat and stir-fry the onions vigorously until softened, about 3 minutes. Add the garlic and ginger and stir-fry 1–2 minutes more until fragrant. Add the crabs and stir-fry vigorously for 5 minutes until they turn bright red.

3 Add all the remaining ingredients, stir for 1–3 minutes more until the gravy has thickened to coat the crab pieces. Serve with chunks of bread or white rice to mop up the gravy.

Note: The character of this simple version of chilli crab changes with the kind of chilli sauce you use. We prefer a plain one like sriracha, as opposed to a sugary, syrupy one like Lingham's. You can even use Fried Chilli Sambal (page 28), which makes the gravy more pungent. If you are squeamish about preparing live crabs, freeze them or blanch them in boiling water for 6 minutes before chopping them up, then fry for 2 minutes only in Step 2.

Malay Sambal Fish

Nothing more than hot white rice and sliced cucumbers on the side is needed to complete this delicious home-style Malay dish.

Serves 4   Cooking time: 20 mins
Preparation time: 10 mins

Oil, for deep-frying
600 g (1⅓ lbs) meaty fish steaks or cutlets
1 tablespoon tamarind pulp
2 tablespoons water
1 tablespoon tomato purée
1 teaspoon sugar
1 teaspoon salt
Juice of 2 limes
Sliced cucumbers, to garnish

Sambal Paste
2 small onions
4 cloves garlic
1 tablespoon dried prawn paste (*belachan*), dry-roasted
6–8 dried red finger-length chillies, soaked until soft

1 Heat the oil in a wok and fry the fish until crisp and golden brown. Set aside to keep warm.

2 Mash the tamarind pulp with the water. Strain to obtain the juice, discarding the solids.

3 Grind all the Sambal Paste ingredients together until fine. Remove all but 4 tablespoons of oil in the wok and stir-fry the Sambal Paste over medium heat for 6–8 minutes. Add the tamarind juice, tomato purée, sugar and salt. Stir for 2 minutes.

4 Return the fish to the wok and stir well to coat the fish with the Sambal. Remove from the heat, drizzle with fresh lime juice and served with sliced cucumbers on the side.

Prawn Sambal

A tasty dish simple enough for everyday—or fancy enough for special occasions, if you use large, fresh tiger prawns. For a more flavourful gravy, leave the prawns' shells and heads on when you fry them.

Serves 4 Cooking time: 12 mins
Preparation time: 15 mins

1½ tablespoons tamarind pulp
3 tablespoons water
6 tablespoons oil
2 teaspoons sugar
2 tablespoons tomato paste
½ teaspoon salt
500 g (1 lb) fresh prawns, peeled
200 g (7 oz) *buah petai* (stinky beans), see note (optional)

Spice Paste
4–6 dried red finger-length chillies, soaked until soft
2 small onions, sliced
5 cloves garlic
1 tablespoon dried prawn paste (*belachan*), dry-roasted

1 Mash the tamarind pulp with the water. Strain to obtain the juice, discarding the solids.

2 Grind all the Spice Paste ingredients together until fine. Heat the oil in a wok over medium heat and stir-fry the Spice Paste for 6–8 minutes until fragrant and thick. Add the tamarind juice, sugar, tomato paste and salt. Bring to a boil.

3 Add the prawns and *buah petai,* if using, and stir-fry for 2–3 minutes or until the prawns are cooked through. Serve hot.

Note: *Buah petai* are small, vivid green beans similar in size to lima beans, with a faint sulphurous flavour that is something of an acquired taste.

Ikan Panggang Barbecued Fish

Just about any firm-fleshed fish can be barbecued in this manner. For more flavour, and to help the fish hold its shape, barbecue the fish whole on the bone rather than using fillets. The delicious sweet-sour soy sauce is what makes this dish work!

Serves 4–5 Cooking time: 16 mins
Preparation time: 10 mins

2 whole fish, about 500 g (1 lb)
Pinch of salt

Sauce
1 tablespoon dried prawn paste (*belachan*)
4 red finger-length chillies, deseeded
2 cloves garlic
3 tablespoons *kecap manis* (thick black sweet soy sauce)
2 tablespoons fresh lime juice

1 To make the Sauce, roast the dried prawn paste over an open flame until crusty (see Sambal Belachan with Kaffir Lime Leaf recipe on page 26). Grind with the chillies and garlic until fine, then mix with the *kecap manis* and lime juice.

2 Pre-heat the grill broiler. Make one or two deep slashes across the thickest part of the fish and sprinkle lightly with salt. Place the fish in a grill pan lined with oiled foil or washed banana leaves. Grill for about 8 minutes on each side, turning once, or until the meat comes away from the bone easily.

3 Spread the Sauce over the grilled fish and serve immediately with boiled rice. Alternatively, serve the Sauce on the side.

Grilled Sambal Stingray

Known as "skate" in the West, stingray is a meaty, succulent fish excellent for grilling or barbecuing. This recipe also works with other firm-textured fish, such as shark or swordfish. Add some oil to the rub if the fish is very lean.

Serves 2–3   Cooking time: 10 mins
Preparation time: 5 mins

600 g (1⅓ lbs) stingray, skin removed
2 tablespoons *kecap manis* (thick black sweet soy sauce)
1 tablespoon ground black pepper
½ teaspoon salt
1 teaspoon sugar
Cut limes and chilli sauce or Fried Chilli Sambal (page 28), to serve

1 Wash the stingray well and pat dry. Mix the *kecap manis*, pepper, salt and sugar together and rub over the stingray.

2 Grill the stingray under a broiler or over hot charcoal, turning once, for 4–5 minutes per side, or until cooked through. Serve hot with cut limes and chilli sauce or Fried Chilli Sambal on the side.

Foo Yong Hai

This dish is otherwise known (and frequently corrupted) as "egg foo yong." If you're in the mood to treat yourself to something really special, substitute crabmeat or scallops for the prawns.

Serves 2–3 Cooking time: 7 mins
Preparation time: 10 mins

1 large carrot
1 ridged loofah (*chi kwa*) or summer squash
5 eggs
4 tablespoons milk
1 tablespoon soy sauce
½ teaspoon ground white pepper
½ teaspoon salt
4 tablespoons oil
2 cloves garlic, crushed
200 g (7 oz) fresh prawns, peeled

1 Peel and slice the carrots into 5 cm (2 in) long matchsticks. Peel the loofah or squash and remove the soft core, then slice into batons.

2 Beat the eggs with the milk, soy sauce, pepper and salt.

3 Heat the oil in a wok over medium heat and stir-fry the garlic for 1 minute, until light brown. Add the carrots and loofah or squash and stir-fry for 3 minutes.

4 Add the prawns and stir-fry for 1½ minutes. Slowly pour in the egg mixture, stirring gently to scramble. When the eggs are softly set, dish up and serve immediately.

Note: The addition of a little milk makes the egg mixture softer and smoother.

Pepper Squid

Nothing could be simpler or faster to prepare than these tender strips of pepper squid.

Serves 2–3   Cooking time: 5 mins
Preparation time: 10 mins

2 large squid (about 500 g/1 lb)
1 tablespoon coarsely ground black pepper
1 teaspoon fine granulated sugar
1 tablespoon cornstarch
Oil, for deep-frying
1 teaspoon salt
Cut limes, to serve

1 Wash the squid. Pull out, cut off and discard the head. Cut the tentacles into small clumps. Slit the body tube down one side and open it out flat. Pull off the skin. Score parallel lines lengthwise along the inside of each body tube, then slice across into thin strips. Pat dry well with paper towels. Mix the squid with the pepper, sugar and cornstarch.

2 Heat the oil in a wok over high heat until it shimmers and gives off a light haze, about 190°C (375°F). Slip the squid into the oil, separating the pieces with chopsticks. Fry in small batches, 45 seconds per batch, until the squid pieces curl up and brown very lightly. Sprinkle with salt and serve with limes on the side.

Note: If you can get hold of baby squid, which are about 4 cm (1½ in) long, use them instead, but deep-fry them until brown and crisp. Serve with sweet flour sauce, hoisin sauce or *kecap manis* (thick black sweet sauce) as a dip.

Grilled Mackerel with Coriander

Mackerel is probably one of the most underrated fish around, maybe because it is inexpensive, and therefore looked askance at, or maybe because it doesn't stay fresh for long (on account of its fish natural oil content). However, its oils, high in omega-3 fatty acids, make it a prime candidate for grilling and are what make this fish so flavourful.

Serves 5–6 Cooking time: 20 mins
Preparation time: 10 mins

3 whole mackerel (about 750 g/1⅔ lbs)
2 teaspoons salt
2 teaspoons ground black pepper
2 tablespoons sunflower oil
3 tablespoons finely chopped fresh coriander
   leaves (cilantro)
Cut limes, to serve

1 Pat each fish dry and make a few deep slashes through the thickest part of the body. Rub all over with the salt, pepper and oil. Place the fish on a grill rack or roasting pan lined with greased foil and cook under a very hot grill or broiler for 6–8 minutes per side, turning once, until cooked through—the fish should feel firm when lightly pressed and the juices should run clear—and the skin is crisp.

2 Sprinkle with chopped coriander leaves and serve with cut limes on the side.

Steamed Pomfret

There are two kinds of pomfret or "angel fish"—and the finer-fleshed white type is better for this traditional Teochew dish. To make it more substantial, scatter thin slices of silken tofu and cooked dried black Chinese mushrooms over and under the fish before steaming it. Don't omit the belly pork—it makes a real difference to the flavour.

Serves 2–4   Cooking time: 9 mins
Preparation time: 10 mins

1 large white pomfret, about 750 g
   (1⅔ lbs), cleaned and gutted
1 tablespoon rendered belly pork oil
1 teaspoon soy sauce
4 preserved sour plums
2 tablespoons finely shredded fresh young ginger root
1 large tomato, cut into 6 wedges
Thinly sliced green onions (scallions), to garnish
Chopped coriander leaves (cilantro), to garnish

1 Score the pomfret 2–3 times on each side and place the fish in a heatproof dish. Drizzle the pork oil and soy sauce over it. Scatter the sour plums, ginger and tomato over the plate.

2 Steam the fish, covered tightly, over high heat for 8–9 minutes or until the fish is cooked through and juices have collected. Serve immediately, garnished with green onions and fresh coriander leaves.

Fish Moolie in Spicy Coconut Sauce

Here fried fish is served in a rich gravy that reflects a blend of Indian and Malay influences. Any meaty fish will do.

Serves 2–3   Preparation time: 20 mins
Cooking time: 13 mins

1 whole red snapper or other firm-fleshed white fish,
    about 500 g (1 lb)
1 teaspoon salt
Oil, for deep-frying
3 tablespoons oil
1½ cups (330 ml) thin coconut milk
1 tablespoon fish sauce
2 tablespoons shredded kaffir lime leaves
2 tomatoes, quartered
1 teaspoon sugar

Spice Paste
1 tablespoon shredded fresh ginger root
2 small onions
2 tablespoons ground coriander
1 tablespoon ground cumin
1 teaspoon ground red pepper

1 Clean and dry the fish thoroughly. Rub with salt. Heat the oil in a wok over medium heat until shimmering, about 200°C (400°F) and deep-fry the fish until crisp and golden brown, 3–4 minutes. Drain the fish on paper towels.

2 Grind all the Spice Paste ingredients together until fine. In a clean wok, heat 3 tablespoons fresh oil and stir-fry the Spice Paste over medium heat for 6 minutes, until thick and fragrant.

3 Add the coconut milk, fish sauce, half the kaffir lime leaves, tomatoes and sugar. Bring to a boil. Add the fish and simmer for another 3 minutes, ladling the sauce over the fish and turning the fish once. Turn over several times to coat liberally. Serve sprinkled with the remaining kaffir lime leaves.

Ikan Masak Pedas Curried Fish

This simple fish curry has a spicy kick—pedas means "hot" in Malay. Increase or reduce the chillies as you wish, for more or less pleasure depending on your taste!

Serves 2–4 Preparation time: 20 mins
Cooking time: 10 mins

600 g (1⅓ lbs) meaty fish steaks or cutlets, like *ikan kurau* or king fish
½ teaspoon salt
2½ tablespoons tamarind pulp
3 cups (750 ml) water
3 tablespoons oil
2 stalks lemongrass, tender inner part of bottom third only, thinly sliced
1 teaspoon sugar
Small handful shredded turmeric leaves (*daun kunyit*)

Spice Paste
3–4 red finger-length chillies
2–3 dried red finger-length chillies, soaked until soft
5 slices galangal root
2 slices fresh turmeric root
5 candlenuts or macadamia nuts
15 Asian shallots
2 teaspoons dried prawn paste (*belachan*), dry-roasted

1 Slice the fish into large chunks and rub with salt. Mash the tamarind pulp with the water. Strain to obtain the juice, discarding the solids.

2 Grind all the Spice Paste ingredients together until fine.

3 Heat the oil in a wok over medium-high heat and stir-fry the Spice Paste vigorously until fragrant, about 4 minutes. Add the tamarind juice, lemongrass and sugar. Bring to a boil, then add the fish and simmer for 6–7 minutes or until the fish is cooked. Garnish with the turmeric leaves and serve.

South Indian Fish Curry

Serve plenty of white rice on the side of this South Indian classic to soak up the sour, hot gravy. You can of course tone down the amount of ground red pepper to taste. For more heft, add some sliced okra, eggplant or tomatoes to the gravy with the fish.

Serves 2–4   Preparation time: 15 mins
Cooking time: 15 mins

2 tablespoons tamarind pulp
1¾ cups (400 ml) water
4 tablespoons oil
1 teaspoon black mustard seeds
1 stalk lemongrass, tender inner part of bottom
   third only, bruised
¾ teaspoon salt
1 teaspoon sugar
600 g (1⅓ lbs) mackerel or swordfish steaks
1 sprig curry leaves

Spice Paste
2 tablespoons ground coriander
1 tablespoon ground cumin
½ teaspoon ground fennel
2 teaspoons ground red pepper
4 slices fresh ginger root
2 cloves garlic
4 Asian shallots

1 Mash the tamarind pulp with the water. Strain to obtain the juice, discarding the solids. Set aside.

2 Grind all the Spice Paste ingredients together until fine. Heat the oil in a wok over medium heat, add the Spice Paste and mustard seeds and stir-fry until fragrant, 5–6 minutes.

3 Add the tamarind juice, lemongrass, salt and sugar. Bring to a boil. Simmer for 4 minutes, then add the fish and curry leaves and simmer for another 6–7 minutes or until the fish is cooked. Serve with white rice.

Sri Lankan Crab Curry

Hailing from Sri Lanka, this curry is usually made with mottled blue flower crabs, which turn bright orange when cooked and have delicate, sweet meat. You can also use stone crabs—the large dark grey-green variety sometimes called "Thunder Crabs." Legend has it that if it nips you with its claws, only a thunderclap will make it release its hold.

Serves 2–4 Preparation time: 20 mins
Cooking time: 30 mins

8 flower crabs or 4 large green crabs
  (about 1.5 kg/3 lbs)
4 tablespoons oil
2½ cups (625 ml) thin coconut milk
1 teaspoon salt
2 tablespoons fresh lime juice
4 tablespoons freshly grated coconut
12 curry leaves

Spice Paste
10 Asian shallots
5 cloves garlic
2 slices fresh ginger root
½ teaspoon ground fenugreek
2 teaspoons ground red pepper
1 teaspoon ground turmeric
½ teaspoon ground cinnamon

1 Remove the carapace of the crabs and discard the lungs and fibrous tissue. Cut the main body into half down the centre line, then cut each half into two pieces. If the claws are large, separate them from the body and crack them lightly with a mallet.

2 Grind all the Spice Paste ingredients together until fine. Heat the oil in a wok over medium heat and stir-fry the Spice Paste for 6 minutes, until fragrant. Add the coconut milk, salt and lime juice. Simmer for 10 minutes.

3 Meanwhile, dry-roast the grated coconut in a dry skillet over low heat until light brown, 3–4 minutes. Add to the curry in the wok and simmer for 5 more minutes, then add the crabs and curry leaves and cook for another 6–8 minutes, stirring frequently, until the crabs are cooked through and the gravy thickens. Serve with rice.

Note: If you are squeamish about preparing live crabs, freeze them or blanch them in boiling water for 6 minutes before chopping them up. After adding them to the curry, cook for 4 minutes only.

Prawns and Squid in Fragrant Coconut Gravy

In its liberal use of lemongrass and galangal, this subtle curry has overtones of northern Malay, Indonesian and Thai cuisines.

Serves 2–4   Preparation time: 20 mins   Cooking time: 15 mins

12 large tiger prawns (about 500 g/1 lb)
200 g (7 oz) squid
6 tablespoons oil
10 Asian shallots, finely sliced
4 green finger-length chillies, each sliced into two
2 tomatoes, halved
1½ cups (375 ml) thin coconut milk
2 tablespoons water
1 tablespoon fish sauce
1 teaspoon sugar

Spice Paste
2 stalks lemongrass, tender inner part of bottom third only, sliced
3 slices galangal root
12 Asian shallots
2–3 red finger-length chillies
5 candlenuts or macadamia nuts
½ tablespoon dried prawn paste (*belachan*), dry-roasted
4 cloves garlic

1 Remove the prawn shells and legs but leave the tails on. Split each prawn down the back and remove the dark vein. Peel off the squid skin. Cut and discard the head but reserve the tentacles. Slice the body tube into rings. Rinse the squid well.

2 Heat 4 tablespoons of the oil in a wok over medium-high heat and stir-fry the shallots, stirring constantly, until golden brown, 2–4 minutes. Remove with a slotted spoon and stir-fry the sliced chillies until soft, 1–2 minutes. Drain both on paper towels and set aside.

3 Grind all the Spice Paste ingredients together until very fine. Add the remaining oil to the wok and stir-fry the Spice Paste for 6 minutes, until thick and fragrant. Add the prawns, squid and all the remaining ingredients and simmer for 4–5 minutes. Garnish with the fried shallots and chillies and serve hot.

Gulai Prawns with Pineapple

This easy and finger-licking good curry is from the Malaysian coastal town of Penang where the word *gulai* is local parlance for "curry."

Serves 3–4 Preparation time: 15 mins
Cooking time: 8 mins

600 g (1⅓ lbs) tiger prawns, washed
4 pieces assam gelugor (dried tamarind)
3 cups (750 ml) water
½ teaspoon salt
1½ teaspoons sugar
300 g (1½ cup) fresh ripe pineapple chunks
Small handful laksa leaves (*daun kesom* or Vietnamese mint)

Spice Paste
6 slices galangal root
1 slice fresh turmeric root
3 candlenuts or macadamia nuts
3–4 red finger-length chillies, deseeded
1 tablespoon dried prawn paste *(belachan)*, dry-roasted

1 Trim the prawns of feelers and legs but leave the shells on. Slit them down the back for easier eating, if preferred. Set aside.

2 Grind all the Spice Paste ingredients together until fine. Combine the Spice Paste and water in a pot and bring to a boil over medium heat. Simmer gently for 3 minutes, then add the assam gelugor, salt, sugar, prawns and pineapple chunks. Simmer uncovered for 5 minutes. Top with laksa leaves and serve.

Kuah Lada Peppery Fish Curry

This Nonya dish of stingray in a tamarind and pepper sauce is spicy and sour and very appetising.

**Serves 4–5 Cooking time: 20 mins
Preparation time: 15 mins**

500 g (1 lb) stingray or baby shark
2 tablespoons tamarind pulp
2½ cups (625 ml) water
4 tablespoons oil
1 teaspoon salt
1 teaspoon sugar
2 long purple Asian eggplants (about 300g/10oz), cut into large batons
2 stalks lemongrass, tender inner part of bottom third only, bruised

Spice Paste
3 red finger-length chillies
6 candlenuts or macadamia nuts
10 Asian shallots
1 thumb-sized piece fresh turmeric root
1 teaspoon black peppercorns
3 slices galangal root

1 Grind all the Spice Paste ingredients together until fine.

2 Cut the fish into large serving pieces.

3 Mash the tamarind pulp with half the amount of water. Strain to obtain the juice, discarding the solids. Mix the tamarind juice with the remaining water.

4 Heat the oil in a wok and stir-fry the Spice Paste over medium heat for 6 minutes, until fragrant. Transfer to a pot and add the tamarind juice, salt and sugar. Bring to a boil. Add the fish, eggplants and lemongrass, then simmer for 10–12 minutes, until the fish is cooked. Serve hot with steamed rice.

Meat

Hainanese Pork Chops

This is an ever-popular local dish which once held sway in British colonial homes and country clubs, prepared by cooks drawn from the Hainanese community. The necessary presence of HP steak sauce in the gravy is a clue.

Serves 3–4   Cooking time: 15 mins
Preparation time: 20 mins

4 thick boneless pork chops
25 cream or saltine crackers
2 large eggs, well beaten
Oil, for deep-frying
2 potatoes, peeled and thickly sliced
1 small onion, sliced
1 tablespoon steak sauce
2 teaspoons soy sauce
1½ tablespoons tomato ketchup
¼ teaspoon salt
2 teaspoons sugar
2 teaspoons cornstarch
⅔ cup (150 ml) water
2 tomatoes, quartered
150 g (1 cup) frozen peas

1 Sandwich the chops between two sheets of plastic wrap and beat lightly with a meat mallet or back end of a meat cleaver to flatten them to a 12-mm (½ -in) thickness.

2 Crush the crackers into fine crumbs. Dip the chops in the egg to coat both sides, then in the cracker crumbs, patting them to form an even layer and shaking off any excess. Repeat the process to obtain a secure, even coating.

3 Heat the oil in a wok until hot, then deep-fry the pork chops two at a time until golden brown, turning once, about 4–6 minutes per batch. Remove and drain well on paper towels.

4 Remove all but 3 tablespoons of the oil from the wok and fry the potatoes over medium heat for 5 minutes, turning frequently, until browned and tender. Remove and drain. Stir-fry the onions in the remaining oil until soft, 2–3 minutes, then add all the remaining ingredients except the tomatoes and peas. Bring to a boil, add the tomatoes, peas and potatoes and simmer for 1 minute, until the sauce thickens. Slice the pork chops and pour the gravy over them to serve.

Note: Crushed crackers are more authentic, but for a crisper coating, use *panko* (Japanese breadcrumbs) which produces a very crisp effect like *tonkatsu*.

Stir-Fried Beef with Kailan

A simple but delicious combination, this dish waits for no one. Cook it quickly and eat it promptly while the *wok hei*—the "breath of the wok"—still wafts from the plate.

Serves 2–3   Cooking time: 6 mins
Preparation time: 15 mins

350 g (12 oz) kailan (Chinese broccoli)
200 g (7 oz) tender beef sirloin
2 teaspoons cornstarch
2 teaspoons soy sauce
3 tablespoons rice wine
2 tablespoons oil
3 cloves garlic, minced
1 tablespoon finely chopped fresh ginger root
2 tablespoons oyster sauce
1 tablespoon sesame oil
1 teaspoon ground black pepper
4 tablespoons water

1 Cut the kailan into 5 cm (2 in) lengths, wash them and drain well. Slice the beef into thin strips and mix with the cornstarch, soy sauce and half the rice wine.

2 Heat the oil in a wok over high heat. Stir-fry the garlic and ginger until golden brown, about 1 minute, then add the beef slices and stir-fry vigorously for 1 minute. Add the kailan and stir-fry for 2 more minutes.

3 Add the remaining rice wine and the rest of the ingredients. Stir-fry for 1–2 minutes more, or until the juices thicken and the kailan is crisp-tender but not overcooked. Serve immediately with rice.

Pork Satay

This recipe is a Chinese spin on the dish popularised by Malay hawker stalls, who use beef, mutton and chicken for their satays and serve the sauce without pineapple. Some culinary scholars trace the word *satay* to the Hokkien *sar tei*, which means "three pieces," a reference to the morsels of meat on the stick.

Serves 4–6 Preparation time: 20 mins plus 5 hours marinating Cooking time: 5–6 mins per batch of satay

30–40 bamboo skewers
750 g (1⅔ lbs) boneless pork rib-eye
2 stalks lemongrass, bruised at root end to make basting brushes
Oil, for basting
Chunkily diced cucumber
Onions and *ketupat* (pressed rice cake), to serve
1 portion Satay Peanut Sauce (page 25), to serve

Marinade
2 tablespoons ground coriander
1 tablespoon ground cumin
1 teaspoon ground fennel
1 teaspoon ground turmeric
6 Asian shallots, finely sliced
2 stalks lemongrass, tender inner part of bottom third only
3 cloves garlic
1 teaspoon salt
1 tablespoon sugar
3 tablespoons oil

1 Make the Satay Peanut Sauce by following the recipe on page 25.

2 Soak the bamboo skewers in cold water for at least 2 hours, to prevent them from burning.

3 Cut the pork into small strips about 2.5 cm (1 in) long and 12 mm (½ in) thick.

4 Grind all the Marinade ingredients to a fine paste and mix with the sliced pork. Let it marinate, covered and refrigerated, at least 5 hours or overnight.

5 Thread 4–5 pieces of the marinated meat on each skewer, pressing them together. Grill the skewers over charcoal or under a very hot broiler for 5–6 minutes, using a lemongrass brush to baste with oil, turning once or twice. Serve hot with the Satay Peanut Sauce, cucumber, onions and *ketupat*.

Tau Yew Bak Soy-Braised Pork

Enormously satisfying in its rustic simplicity, this is the perfect dish to eat with rice congee.

Serves 3–4 Cooking time: 1 hour 5 mins
Preparation time: 10 mins

2 tablespoons oil
2 tablespoons fine granulated sugar
600 g (1⅓ lbs) pork leg, skin on, cut into bite-sized chunks
6 cloves garlic, lightly smashed
2½ cups (625 ml) water
5 tablespoons thick dark soy sauce
½ teaspoon salt
1 large walnut-sized knob of galangal or ginger root, peeled and bruised

1 Heat the oil and sugar together in a wok over medium heat, stirring frequently. Watch it like a hawk; when the sugar has melted and caramelised into little brown globules, add the pork—the caramel will splutter—and stir vigorously.

2 Add all the remaining ingredients, bring to a boil, cover and simmer for 1 hour, stirring occasionally, or until the pork is fork tender. Serve hot.

Note: Treacly thick dark soy sauce is the best to use for this dish, but if you cannot get it, use regular dark soy sauce.

Beef Rendang

This classic Indonesian curry was originally made with water buffalo. It is up to you how much to reduce the sauce. You can cook it until the beef is bathed with a thick gravy— at which stage it is called *kalio*—or further until it is almost dry in true *rendang* style, in which case you must stir constantly near the end to prevent scorching.

Serves 2–4   Preparation time: 15 mins
Cooking time: 1¾ to 2 hours

1 kg (2 lbs) rump or stewing beef, cut into large chunks
3½ cups (825 ml) thin coconut milk
3 stalks lemongrass, tender inner part of bottom third only
6 kaffir lime leaves
4 slices galangal root
1 teaspoon salt

Spice Paste
5 tablespoons freshly grated coconut
6–8 dried red finger-length chillies, soaked until soft
2 tablespoons ground coriander
1 tablespoon ground turmeric
1 teaspoon ground cumin
1 small onion, chopped
5 slices fresh ginger root

1 To prepare the Spice Paste, dry-roast the grated coconut in a dry wok or skillet over medium-low heat, stirring constantly, until it turns light brown, 5–6 minutes. Grind with the remaining Spice Paste ingredients until fine.

2 Combine the Spice Paste with the beef and all the other ingredients in a large heavy-based pot and bring to a boil over medium heat. Reduce the heat to low, partially cover and simmer for 1½ –2 hours or until the beef is tender and the gravy is very thick and shiny with oil. Serve hot.

Note: This keeps for a couple of weeks in the fridge, tightly covered. Use a clean spoon to dish it out as the coconut will spoil if contaminated. It also freezes very well.

Devil Curry

This is Chris' version of a quintessential festive recipe, also known as "curry debal," from the Singapore's illustrious community, descendants of the Portuguese who sailed to Goa in India, Galle in Sri Lanka and Malacca in Malaysia in the sixteenth century. It is very hot, very substantial and irresistible.

Serves 6–7 Preparation time: 30 mins
Cooking time: 1 hour 45 mins

1 large chicken, cut into portions
1 tablespoon soy sauce
1 tablespoon dark soy sauce
20–30 dried red finger-length chillies, soaked until soft
3 stalks lemongrass, tender inner part of bottom third only, thinly sliced
8 cloves garlic
3 small onions, peeled
6 slices fresh galangal
2 slices fresh turmeric root
½ cup (125 ml) oil
8 slices fresh ginger root
2 teaspoons black mustard seeds
2 small onions, peeled and quartered
6 tomatoes, quartered
3 cups (750 ml) water
250 g (8 oz) Chinese roast pork with crackling (*siew yok*), cut into chunks
4 smoked sausages (such as bockwurst), cut into chunks
3 tablespoons powdered hot mustard
⅓ cup (80 ml) vinegar
½ head cabbage, cut into large pieces
Salt, to taste
Sugar, to taste

Toppings
2 tablespoons oil
1 small onion, sliced
2 red finger-length chillies, deseeded and thinly sliced diagonally
3 tablespoons thinly sliced fresh ginger root

1 Toss the chicken with the soy sauces to coat, then place in an oiled roasting pan and roast for 40 minutes in a preheated oven at 190°C (375°F).

2 Grind the soaked chillies to a paste with the lemongrass and garlic. Set aside. Grind the onions, galangal and turmeric together into a paste and set aside.

3 Heat the oil in a large wok over medium-low heat. When hot, add the chilli paste and stir-fry, stirring constantly, 8–10 minutes or until slightly darkened and the "raw" smell has dissipated. Spoon the paste into a bowl, leaving the oil in the pan. Add the onion paste, ginger and mustard seeds to the pan and stir-fry 6–7 minutes, stirring constantly, until thick and fragrant.

4 Return the chilli paste to the wok and stir-fry for 1 more minute, then add the chicken, together with their juices and browned bits in the roasting pan, onions, tomatoes and water. Bring to a boil and simmer for 15 minutes, then add the roast pork, smoked sausage, mustard and vinegar. Simmer for 15 more minutes, then add the cabbage. Cook for another 6–8 minutes or until the cabbage is tender, season with salt and sugar to taste.

5 To make the Toppings, heat the oil over high heat, add the onions, chillies and ginger. Toss until lightly browned, 2–3 minutes. Sprinkle it over the curry to serve.

Note: Add some bacon bones in step 4 to make this even more authentic. Once fully cooled, store in an airtight container in the fridge, where it will keep for at least a week. Scoop what you want to eat with a clean spoon and bring to a full boil before serving.

Pork Ribs and Bamboo Shoot Curry

Bamboo shoots gives this very cross-cultural dish a distinctive flavour and crunch.

Serves 3–4 Cooking time: 50 mins
Preparation time: 10 mins

3 tablespoons oil
600 g (1⅓ lbs) pork ribs, cut into 5-cm (2-in) chunks
200 g (1¼ cups) sliced fresh or frozen bamboo shoots
2½ cups (625 ml) thin coconut milk
1 teaspoon salt
1 teaspoon sugar

Spice Paste
6–8 dried red finger-length chillies, soaked until soft
3 thin slices galangal root
1 tablespoon dried prawn paste (*belachan*), dry-roasted
1 thumb-sized piece fresh turmeric root
2 tablespoons ground coriander
1 teaspoon ground black pepper

1 Grind all the Spice Paste ingredients together until fine. Heat the oil in a wok over medium-low heat and stir-fry the Spice Paste, stirring constantly, until thick and fragrant, 6–8 minutes.

2 Add all the other ingredients to the wok, bring to a boil and simmer over medium-low heat, partially covered, for 45 minutes or until the pork ribs are very tender. Serve hot.

Ngoh Hiang Pork and Crab Rolls

Peranakans, Teochews and Hokkiens all have their own spins on this deep-fried meat roll. We say *vive la différence!*

Serves 6–8 Cooking time: 20 mins
Preparation time: 20 mins

200 g (¾ cup) fresh shelled prawn
   meats
400 g (2 cups) fresh ground pork
6 water chestnuts, peeled and diced
1 clove garlic, finely chopped
2 Asian shallots, finely sliced
2 teaspoons rice wine
1 teaspoon soy sauce
½ teaspoon sugar
¾ teaspoon salt
150 g (1½ cups) cooked crabmeat
2 sheets dried tofu skin
1 tablespoon cornstarch, dissolved in
   1 tablespoon water
Oil, for deep-frying
Sweet flour sauce, hoisin sauce or
   kecap manis (thick black sweet soy
   sauce) and bottled sweet chilli sauce,
   to serve

1 Coarsely chop the prawn meat and mix with with the pork, water chestnuts, garlic and shallots until well blended. Sprinkle with the rice wine, soy sauce, sugar and salt. Mix well. Gently mix in the crabmeat and set aside.

2 Trim off the thick edges of the dried tofu skins. Cut the sheets into six rectangles 23 cm x 30 cm (9 in x 12 in) and rinse them quickly under running water to remove any oil or salt. Gently pat the skins dry.

3 Lay 1 sheet of tofu skin on a clean work surface. Place 3 tablespoons of the filling along one shorter edge and shape it into a log, leaving a small margin at each end. Roll the skin around the filling, tucking in the sides as you go. Smear a little cornstarch solution along the end and press to seal. Repeat with the remaining skins and filling.

4 Place the rolls in a lightly greased steamer tray, spacing them at least 12 mm (½ in) apart. Steam over high heat for 9 minutes, or until just cooked. Transfer the rolls to a lightly oiled plate and set aside to cool.

5 Heat the oil in a wok until very hot and just starting to shimmer. Fry the rolls in batches of 3 or 4; carefully lower the rolls into the oil and fry, turning occasionally, until golden brown all over. Remove and drain on paper towels. Slice the rolls into bite-size pieces. Serve with sweet flour sauce, hoisin sauce or *kecap manis* and chilli sauce for dipping.

Babi Assam Tamarind Pork

Though this dish is traditionally made with belly pork, you can use any cut of pork, just so long as it includes a little fat—essential for the flavour and texture. This keeps, tightly covered, in the fridge for at least a week. But it never lasts that long in our house.

Serves 4–5 Cooking time: 1 hour 10 mins
Preparation time: 15 mins

2½ tablespoons tamarind pulp
1¾ cups (425 ml) water
5 tablespoons oil
1 tablespoon salted fermented soybean paste (*tau cheo*), mashed
700 g (1½ lbs) boneless pork rib-eye, cubed
2 stalks lemongrass, tender inner part of bottom third only, bruised
3 tablespoons shaved palm sugar or dark brown sugar
Salt to taste
½ ginger bud (*bunga kantan*), very thinly sliced

Spice Paste
10 Asian shallots
4 candlenuts or macadamia nuts
6 slices fresh galangal root
3 cloves garlic
1 thumb-sized piece fresh turmeric root
2 slices fresh ginger root
2 dried red finger-length chillies
2–4 red finger-length chillies
1 teaspoon dried prawn paste (*belachan*), dry-roasted

1 Mash the tamarind pulp with the water. Strain to obtain the juice, discarding the solids. Set aside.

2 Grind all the Spice Paste ingredients together until fine. Heat the oil in a wok over medium heat and stir-fry the Spice Paste, stirring constantly, for 6–8 minutes or until the paste is fragrant and has reduced in volume by about a third.

3 Add the salted fermented soybean paste and stir-fry for 1 minute, then add the pork, lemongrass and tamarind juice. Stir well. Simmer for 1 hour, partially covered, until the pork is tender and the gravy has thickened. Stir in the palm sugar and salt to taste. Garnish with the shredded ginger bud and serve hot with plain steamed rice.

Babi Chin Sweet Soy Pork

There are several cultures in this sweet, aromatic dish: Indian, Chinese and Thai principally. If you have time, dry-roast coriander seeds until fragrant and grind them fresh for this dish—it really makes a difference!

Serves 4–6   Cooking time: 45 mins
Preparation time: 15 mins

2 heaping tablespoons ground coriander (from freshly dry-roasted and ground coriander seeds)
2 tablespoons cold water
4 tablespoons oil
15 Asian shallots, finely sliced
8 cloves garlic, finely minced
3 tablespoons salted fermented soybean paste (*tau cheo*), mashed
500 g (1 lb) boneless pork shoulder, cut into large chunks
3 tablespoons thick dark soy sauce
1 teaspoon salt
1½ tablespoons sugar
½ teaspoon ground cinnamon
½ teaspoon ground cloves
4 cups (1 litre) water
150 g (1 cup) bamboo shoots, cut into small pieces
3–4 green finger-length chillies

1 Mix the ground coriander with the water to form a wet paste.

2 Heat the oil in a wok over medium heat and stir-fry the shallots for 3 minutes, stirring constantly, then add the garlic and stir-fry for 2 more minutes. Add the coriander paste and salted fermented soybean paste. Stir well for 2 minutes.

3 Remove and transfer the pork to a large pot along with the thick dark soy sauce, salt, sugar, cinnamon, clove and water. Simmer for 30 minutes. Add the bamboo shoots and simmer for 10 more minutes, until the gravy is thick and aromatic. Break the green chillies into rough pieces and mix them in, then serve immediately.

Sambal Spiced Pork

This mouth-watering pork is as good in a sandwich as it is with white rice. This keeps well refrigerated and covered airtight, and in fact tastes better the next day.

Serves 4–5 Cooking time: 30 mins
Preparation time: 15 mins

1.5 kg (3 lbs) belly pork, skin removed
4 tablespoons oil
1 tablespoon sugar
1 teaspoon salt
2 tablespoons dark soy sauce
4 kaffir lime leaves, shredded (optional)

Spice Paste
6 cloves garlic
20 Asian shallots
8 candlenuts or macadamia nuts
2 stalks lemongrass, tender inner part of bottom third only, sliced
4 slices galangal root
6–8 dried red finger-length chillies, soaked until soft
1 tablespoon dried prawn paste (*belachan*), dry-roasted

1 Slice the belly pork thickly. Blanch the pork slices in a large pot of boiling water for 8 minutes, then drain well and cut into bite-sized chunks.

2 Grind all the Spice Paste ingredients together until fine. Heat the oil in a wok over medium-low heat and stir-fry the Spice Paste until thick and fragrant, 7–8 minutes.

3 Add the pork, sugar, salt and soy sauce, reduce the heat to low and stir-fry for 15 minutes, stirring constantly. Add a little water if necessary to prevent the pork from scorching. When done, the pork should be tender and coated with a very thick sauce. Mix in the shredded kaffir lime leaves just before serving.

Babi Goreng Satay Fried Pork

The addition of kaffir lime leaves gives this pan-fried variation of skewered satay a fragrant twist. We can thank Nonya cooks for giving us license to cook satay in a frying pan.

Serves 4   Cooking time: 35 mins
Preparation time: 15 mins

3 tablespoons oil
600 g (1⅓ lbs) boneless pork ribs, marbled with a
   little fat, thinly sliced
1¾ cups (415 ml) thin coconut milk
4 kaffir lime leaves
1 teaspoon salt
2 teaspoons sugar

Spice Paste
3 stalks lemongrass, tender inner part of bottom
   third only
3–5 red finger-length chillies
5 candlenuts or macadamia nuts
10 Asian shallots
1 tablespoon dried prawn paste (*belachan*),
   dry-roasted
1 teaspoon ground turmeric
2 tablespoons ground coriander
1 teaspoon ground cumin
1 teaspoon ground fennel

1 To make the Spice Paste, grind all the ingredients together to form a thick paste. Add a little water if necessary, to keep the blades turning. Heat the oil and stir-fry the Spice Paste for 4 minutes until fragrant and the oil oozes out. Add the pork slices and continue to stir-fry for 3 more minutes.

2 Stir in the coconut milk, kaffir lime leaves, salt and sugar. Bring to a boil over medium heat, stirring constantly until the gravy is thick and aromatic.

3 Remove from the heat, discard the kaffir lime leaves. Garnish with the sliced chillies, if desired, and serve with plain steamed rice.

Vegetables

Spicy Okra with Prawns

Okra (or ladies' fingers as they are known here) is a versatile vegetable by virtue of its succulent plainness. It makes a fine addition to many curries and is wonderful simply steamed whole and eaten with spicy sambal and fresh lime juice.

Serves 3–4   Cooking time: 10 mins
Preparation time: 15 mins

16 stems okra (about 250 g/8 oz total)
3 tablespoons oil
300 g (10 oz) fresh prawns, peeled
1 teaspoon salt
2 tablespoons fresh lime juice
5 tablespoons water
1 teaspoon sugar

Spice Paste
3 red finger-length chillies, deseeded
8–10 Asian shallots
2 stalks lemongrass, tender inner part of bottom third only, sliced
6 candlenuts or macadamia nuts
1 scant teaspoon dried prawn paste (*belachan*), dry-roasted
¾ teaspoon ground turmeric

1 Trim off the okra stems and pointed tips. Cut the okra into bite-sized lengths and blanch them in boiling water for 1½ minutes, then drain well and rinse with cold water. This helps to reduce the stickiness.

2 Grind all the Spice Paste ingredients together until fine. Heat the oil in a wok over medium-high heat and stir-fry the Spice Paste until thick and fragrant, 3–4 minutes.

3 Add the okra and stir-fry for 1 minute, then add all the remaining ingredients and fry for 3–4 minutes until the prawns are cooked through. Serve immediately.

Lohan Chai Buddha's Vegetarian Feast

Sometimes called "Buddha's Delight" on Chinese restaurant menus, this is a simplified version of the original recipe, which contains eighteen ingredients that symbolise Buddha's eighteen disciples. This dish is traditionally served on the eve of Chinese New Year and is appreciated for its flavour by any Chinese household, whatever their religion.

Serves 4–6 Cooking time: 35 mins Preparation time: 20 mins

20 snow peas, tops and tails trimmed
20 green beans, sliced
1 large carrot, thinly sliced
12 dried black Chinese mushrooms, soaked in hot water 1
    hour, stems discarded, caps halved
1 can (425-g/15-oz) straw mushrooms, drained
1 can (397-g/14-oz) ginkgo nuts, drained
1 can (440-g/15-oz) lotus seeds, drained
¼ head Chinese (Napa) cabbage, cut into broad strips
4 pieces sweet dried tofu strips (*tau kee*)
Small handful of black moss fungus (*fatt choi*)
4 tablespoons oil
3 cloves garlic, crushed
5 slices fresh ginger root
3 cubes fermented red tofu (*lam yee*)
2 tablespoons hoisin sauce
2 tablespoons soy sauce
4 cups (1 litre) water

1 Wash and cut all the vegetables into bite-sized pieces. Rinse and thoroughly drain the straw mushrooms, ginkgo nuts and lotus seeds. Rinse the sweet tofu strips in warm water and snip them into 12-mm (½-in) wide strips with scissors. Soak the black moss fungus in tepid water for 5 minutes, then drain well.

2 Heat the oil in a wok over high heat and stir-fry the garlic and ginger for 1–2 minutes, until fragrant. Reduce the heat to low and add the fermented red tofu. Mash it lightly with the back of the wok spatula, then add the hoisin sauce, soy sauce and all the vegetables. Stir well and add the water. Bring to a boil and simmer for 25–30 minutes or until the gravy is rich and thick and the vegetables are tender. Serve hot.

Note: This can keep for several days refrigerated. Reheat fully to serve.

Bean Sprouts with Tofu

Elegant in its simplicity, this vegetarian stir-fry takes little time to prepare. For best results, use the freshest sprouts and garlic chives that you can find.

Serves 2–3 Cooking time: 6 mins
Preparation time: 10 mins

150 g (3 cups) fresh bean sprouts
½ cake (150 g/5 oz) pressed tofu (*tau kwa*)
1 tablespoon oil
2 cloves garlic, minced
100 g (2½ cups) Chinese chives (garlic chives or *koo chai*), cut into short lengths
¾ teaspoon salt

1 Rinse and pat dry the bean sprouts. Nip off the roots and remove any brown seed caps. Dice the pressed tofu.

2 Heat the oil in a wok over high heat and stir-fry the garlic for 1 minute or until lightly browned. Add the diced pressed tofu and stir-fry, stirring gently, for 2–3 minutes, until browned all over. Add all the other ingredients and stir-fry vigorously for 2 minutes until the vegetables are cooked. Serve immediately.

Spicy Long Beans

This is a standard item seen at Chinese and Malay cooked-food hawker stalls. Any kind of long bean and even asparagus can be cooked this way.

Serves 3–4 Cooking time: 15 mins Preparation time: 10 mins

15 long beans or 30–40 green beans
4 tablespoons oil
1 tablespoon fish sauce
1 teaspoon sugar
¼ cup (60 ml) water

Spice Paste
1 stalk lemongrass, tender inner part of bottom third only
3 slices galangal root
2–3 red finger-length chillies, deseeded
5 candlenuts or macadamia nuts
1 tablespoon dried prawn paste (*belachan*), dry-roasted
8–10 Asian shallots
5 cloves garlic

1 Cut the long beans into short lengths, wash and drain.

2 Grind all the Spice Paste ingredients together until fine. Heat the oil in a wok over medium heat and stir-fry the Spice Paste until thick and fragrant, 5–7 minutes.

3 Add the long beans, fish sauce and sugar. Stir-fry for 5–7 minutes, until the beans are tender. Sprinkle the water over as you fry—you may not need all of it. When done the beans should be moist but not swimming in liquid. Serve with hot rice.

Kangkong Belachan

Made with garlic, chillies and dried prawn paste, this dish of stir-fried water spinach is packed with flavour. Western spinach, or any other quick-cooking leafy vegetable, can be used for this recipe.

Serves 3–4 Cooking time: 8 mins Preparation time: 15 mins

250 g (8 oz) *kangkong* (water spinach)
1 tablespoon dried prawn paste (*belachan*), dry-roasted
2 tablespoons dried prawns, soaked in water until soft
3–4 red finger-length chillies, deseeded
4 cloves garlic
3–4 tablespoons oil
⅔ cup (165 ml) water

1 Cut off and discard the tough ends of the *kangkong* stems. Slice the remaining stalks into 7.5 cm (3 in) lengths, then rinse well in a basin of cold water to remove any grit.

2 Grind the dried prawn paste with the dried prawns, chillies and garlic until fine. Heat the oil in a wok over medium-high heat and stir-fry the paste vigorously for 3–4 minutes until fragrant.

3 Add the *kangkong* and stir-fry for 2 minutes, then add the water and stir for 1 more minute. Serve immediately.

Pumpkin with Dried Prawns

This is a very old-fashioned Chinese recipe. Japanese *kabocha* squash, Australian blue-skinned pumpkin, or American butternut squash work well with this recipe—in fact often better than our local brown pumpkins, which can be watery.

Serves 3–4   Cooking time: 17 mins
Preparation time: 15 mins

1 small pumpkin or butternut squash, about 20–25 cm
   (about 8–10 in) across (1.5 kg/3 lbs)
1 tablespoon oil
4 cloves garlic, minced
1½ tablespoons dried prawns, soaked until soft
2 tablespoons rice wine
¾ cup (190 ml) chicken or pork stock or water
2 teaspoons soy sauce
¾ teaspoon salt

1 Slice the pumpkin or squash into thick wedges (about 3-cm/1¼-in thick). Cut away and discard the skin, seeds and fibres, then cut each wedge into 3 pieces.

2 Heat the oil in a wok over medium heat. Add the garlic and stir-fry for 1 minute, then add the dried prawns and stir-fry for 1 more minute. Add the rice wine, stock or water, soy sauce, salt and pumpkin. Bring to a boil, then partially cover and reduce the heat to medium-low. Simmer, stirring frequently, until the pumpkin is tender and the gravy reduces to a couple of spoonfuls, 10–15 minutes.

Nangka Lemak Young Jackfruit Curry

Sold in bags in Malay vegetable stalls, unripe jackfruit, or *nangka muda*, is pale green, firm and tart. As it ripens it turns yellow and becomes easier to separate into lobes of crisp-textured flesh.

Serves 4–6   Cooking time: 30 mins
Preparation time: 20 mins

1 kg (2 lbs) unripe jackfruit (*nangka muda*), skin discarded
1 teaspoon salt
4 tablespoons oil
2½ cups (625 ml) thin coconut milk
200 g (7 oz) fresh prawns, peeled
2 tablespoons fish sauce
2 teaspoons sugar

Spice Paste
3 tablespoons dried prawns, soaked in warm water until soft
2 stalks lemongrass, tender inner part of bottom third only, sliced
6–8 red finger-length chillies
6 candlenuts or macadamia nuts
2 small onions
1 tablespoon dried prawn paste (*belachan*), dry-roasted
1 thumb-size piece fresh turmeric root

1 Slice the jackfruit into large chunks. Bring a large pot of water to a boil. Add the jackfruit and salt and simmer for 15 minutes or until the fruit is tender. Drain and rinse the jackfruit with cold water. Set aside.

2 Grind all the Spice Paste ingredients together until fine. Heat the oil in a wok over medium heat and stir-fry the Spice Paste for about 6 minutes, until thick and fragrant. Add the coconut milk and jackfruit and simmer for 7–8 minutes.

3 Add the prawns and cook for 2 minutes. Stir in the fish sauce and sugar. Serve hot with rice.

Eggplant Sambal

Eggplants (brinjals, as they are locally known) come in all shapes and sizes. The most common ones locally are the slim purple eggplants about 30 cm (1 foot) long, though the shorter ones (about 13 cm/5 in long) and the fat, black-purple ones more common in the West can be used for this dish too.

Serves 2–3 Cooking time: 10 mins
Preparation time: 10 mins

1 tablespoon tamarind pulp
4 tablespoons water
6 tablespoons oil
⅓ teaspoon salt
1 tablespoon sugar
1 tablespoon tomato paste
2 long purple Asian eggplants (about 300g/10oz each), or 5 small ones

Spice Paste
4–6 dried red finger-length chillies, soaked until soft
2 small onions
6 cloves garlic
1 tablespoon dried prawn paste (*belachan*), dry-roasted

1 Mash the tamarind pulp with the water. Strain to obtain the juice, discarding the solids.

2 Grind all the Spice Paste ingredients together until fine. Heat the oil in a wok over medium heat. Stir-fry the Spice Paste for 5–6 minutes or until fragrant, then add the tamarind juice, salt, sugar and tomato paste. Cook for 1 minute more. Remove and keep warm.

3 Halve the eggplants lengthwise. If using big ones, cut each half into three pieces. Cook the eggplants as desired (see note below). Pour the Spice Paste mixture over the eggplants and serve hot.

Note: Eggplants are tastiest flash-fried in hot oil until tender, but the result is somewhat greasy. You can also pan-fry them with a little oil in a non-stick pan over high heat, turning frequently, or blanch or steam them for 2–3 minutes, until soft.

Sayur Lodeh Mixed Vegetable Stew

This very simple yet tasty vegetable stew is mandatory at every *nasi padang* (Malay rice and cooked dishes) stall. Serve it with compressed rice slices (*lemang*) and *serondeng* for a complete meal.

Serves 3–4 Cooking time: 20 mins
Preparation time: 10 mins

1 long Asian eggplant (about 300 g/10 oz)
12–15 green beans, tops and tails trimmed
2 small carrots
¼ head of cabbage, sliced
5 tablespoons oil
2 cups (500 ml) thin coconut milk
¾ cup (190 ml) water
1 teaspoon salt
1 teaspoon sugar

Spice Paste
6 candlenuts or macadamia nuts
8–10 Asian shallots
2 teaspoons dried prawn paste (*belachan*), dry-roasted
1 teaspoon dried prawns, soaked until soft
1 thumb-sized piece fresh turmeric root
3 cloves garlic
4–6 red finger-length chillies

1 Halve the eggplant lengthwise and slice into segments about 12 mm (½ in) thick. Slice the beans diagonally in half, slice the carrots into 4-cm (1½-in) sticks and the cabbage into wide strips.

2 Grind all the Spice Paste ingredients together until fine. Heat the oil in a wok over medium heat and stir-fry the Spice Paste until fragrant, 4–5 minutes. Add the coconut milk and water and bring to a boil. Add all the vegetables and simmer for 10 minutes.

3 Add the salt and sugar and simmer for 5 more minutes or until the vegetables are tender. Serve hot.

Desserts

Nonya Pineapple Tarts

These rich Chinese New Year delicacies originally have Portuguese origins, but are now loved by all; in Malacca, the Nonya, Eurasian, Chitty and Malay communities all make different versions. Rather than the traditional grated fresh pineapple, we prefer to use canned pineapple in natural juice as it is consistently ripe and flavourful.

Makes 2–3 dozen tarts   Cooking time: 2 hours plus 20 mins baking time (per batch)
Preparation time: 45 mins per batch plus   20 mins chilling time

Pineapple Jam
2 cans (450 g/1 lb each) unsweetened pineapple chunks in natural juice
½ pod star anise, broken into pieces
2 cinnamon sticks
3 cloves
250 g (1¼ cups) fine granulated sugar, plus more as needed

Pastry
200 g (1⅓ cups) plain flour, sifted
1 tablespoon fine granulated sugar
½ teaspoon salt
125 g (½ cup) unsalted butter, cubed
2 egg yolks
1 teaspoon vanilla essence
2 tablespoons iced water
1 egg, beaten with 1 tablespoon water

Tart
1 egg, beaten with 1 tablespoon water
Whole cloves

1 To make the Pineapple Jam, drain the pineapple, reserving the juice. Chop very finely in a food processor. Combine with the juice, spices and sugar in a pot (non-aluminium, preferably non-stick). Stir well over medium heat until the sugar completely dissolves. Taste, and add more sugar as needed for a tart-sweet balance. Bring to a boil, reduce the heat to medium-low and cook, stirring frequently, until the mixture is reduced to a thick, amber-coloured jam, 1½ –2½ hours. Watch it carefully towards the end, stirring to prevent scorching. Let cool completely. Store in an airtight container in the fridge.

2 Make the Pastry by whisking the flour, sugar and salt together in a large mixing bowl until well blended. Add the butter and rub them in with your fingertips or a pastry whisk, until the mixture resembles fine breadcrumbs. Beat the egg yolks, vanilla extract and water together and drizzle evenly over the flour mixture. Stir with a fork to bring the dough together into a ball. Knead lightly for a few seconds, divide the dough into three portions. Wrap in plastic wrap and chill in the fridge for 1 hour.

3 To make the Tart, work with one third of a Pastry batch at a time. Pinch off a large walnut-sized piece of Pastry and flatten it to about 4 mm (⅛ in) thickness with your fingers to form a disk. Place 1 teaspoon of the Pineapple Jam on each disk and pull up the edges to enclose the jam. Pinch off any excess Pastry and roll the ball between your palms to make it round. Brush the tart with the egg mixture to glaze and stick a clove into it. If you like, use a small pair of scissors to snip tiny 'v's in the Pastry to make the Tart resemble a pineapple. Repeat with the remaining Pastry and Pineapple Jam.

4 Place the tarts on a baking sheet lined with baking paper and bake in a preheated oven at 170°C (340°F) for 20–25 minutes or until golden brown. If the tarts brown too fast, lower the heat to 160°C (325°F) halfway through. When done, cool on a rack before placing in an airtight container.

Coconut Pancakes with Banana Sauce

This recipe has Indonesian and Peranakan roots. The contrast of light, spongy pancakes with a rich banana sauce is irresistible. Use ripe creamy-textured bananas for best results.

Serves 5–6   Cooking time: 40 mins (approx)
Preparation time: 10 mins plus 3 hours standing time

Pancakes
250 g (2 cups) rice flour
¼ cup (60 ml) water
1 cup (250 ml) coconut water, or plain water mixed with
    2 teaspoons sugar
2¼ teaspoons active dried yeast
1 tablespoon sugar
3 tablespoons flour
2 tablespoons glutinous rice flour
¾ teaspoon salt
⅔ cup (150 ml) coconut milk
Oil, to grease the griddle

Banana Sauce
100 g (½ cup) shaved palm sugar or dark brown sugar
3 tablespoons fine granulated sugar
⅜ cup (100 ml) water
2 pandanus leaves, tied into a knot
1¼ cups (310 ml) thin coconut milk
2 teaspoons glutinous rice flour, dissolved in 2 tablespoons water
½ teaspoon salt
5 ripe bananas, peeled and sliced

1 To make the Pancakes, combine 2 tablespoons of the rice flour and the water in a pan and cook over low heat, stirring constantly, until the mixture thickens to a paste. Transfer to a large mixing bowl and whisk in the remaining rice flour, coconut water, yeast, sugar, flour and glutinous rice flour. Let stand at cool room temperature for 2 hours or until it becomes frothy and doubles in volume. Then whisk in the coconut milk and let stand for 1 more hour.

2 To make the Banana Sauce, bring the palm sugar, sugar, water and pandanus leaves to a boil in a pot over medium heat, stirring to dissolve the sugar. Add the coconut milk, glutinous rice flour mixture, salt and bananas and cook, stirring occasionally, for 6 minutes or until the bananas are just tender. Turn off the heat and set aside.

3 Lightly stir the batter. Heat a pancake griddle over medium-low heat (preferably on a wide burner). Grease with oil. When hot, ladle small amounts of batter (about 2 tablespoons for each pancake) onto the griddle to form small pancakes about 8 cm (3 in) across. Cook for 2–3 minutes on each side and transfer the cooked Pancakes to a plate. You should get 20–22 pancakes in total. Serve hot with the Banana Sauce.

Indian Rice Pudding

A payasam is a milk-based dessert of which there are many variations, hailing from all over India. This one is thickened with rice. You can substitute jaggery (Indian palm sugar) for half the sugar for a caramel-like flavour.

Serves 4–5   Cooking time: 50 mins
Preparation time: 5 mins

4 cups (1 litre) milk
90 g (½ cup) uncooked basmati rice,
   rinsed and drained
3 cardamom pods, lightly crushed
¼ teaspoon ground nutmeg
100 g (½ cup) sugar
2 tablespoons ghee or butter
100 g (¾ cup) raw cashew nuts
4 tablespoons raisins
Pinch of ground cardamom

1 Bring the milk to a boil in a large heavy-based saucepan over medium heat, stirring occasionally. Add the basmati rice, cardamom and nutmeg. Return to a boil. Reduce the heat to low and cook, partially covered, for about 40 minutes or until the rice is soft, stirring frequently. When the rice is done, stir in the sugar until it completely dissolves. Switch off the heat, cover and set aside.

2 Melt the ghee or butter in a small frying pan over medium-low heat. Add the cashew nuts and raisins and stir-fry until the nuts are lightly browned, 4–5 minutes. Stir the nuts and raisins into the pudding, reserving a few for garnish. Serve the pudding hot or cold, garnished with the reserved nuts, raisins and a sprinkle of ground cardamom on top.

Kueh Dadar Coconut Filled Pancakes

Though baking powder is untraditional, we like to add a little bit to help make the pancakes softer and lighter. These do not keep well and are best eaten fresh.

Makes 20 pancakes   Cooking time: 40 mins
Preparation time: 15 mins plus 15 mins standing time

Pancakes
100 g (⅔ cup) cake flour, sifted
100 g (⅔ cup) plain flour, sifted
1½ tablespoons fine granulated sugar
½ teaspoon salt
1¾ cups (425 ml) thin coconut milk
5 tablespoons Pandanus Juice (see note)
1 large egg
½ teaspoon baking powder

Coconut Filling
175 g (¾ cup) shaved palm sugar or dark brown sugar, finely chopped
4 tablespoons fine granulated sugar
⅓ cup (80 ml) water
2 pandanus leaves, tied into a knot
⅓ teaspoon salt
250 g (2½ cups) fresh grated coconut

1 To make the Coconut Filling, combine both sugars with the water, pandanus leaves and salt in a saucepan and cook over low heat, stirring constantly, until the sugar completely dissolves. Strain into a clean pan and add the grated coconut. Continue to cook, stirring constantly, over medium-low heat for 5–7 minutes, or until the coconut has absorbed all the liquid and formed moist, juicy clumps. Set aside to cool.

2 To make the Pancakes, combine both flours, sugar and salt in a mixing bowl. Whisk the coconut milk, Pandanus Juice and egg together and slowly whisk this into the flour mixture until smooth. Let the batter stand for 15 minutes at room temperature. Whisk in the baking powder just before you begin to fry the pancakes.

3 Lightly grease a non-stick frying pan and set it over medium-low heat. Spoon 2–3 tablespoons of batter into the pan and tilt the pan to spread the batter into a thin pancake. Cook for 45 seconds or until the edges look dry, then flip and cook 40 seconds more or until set and cooked. Transfer to a plate and repeat with the remaining batter. The Pancakes should blister but barely brown at all.

4 To assemble, lay a Pancake on a plate. Stir the Coconut Filling and place 1 tablespoon near the edge of the Pancake, then roll it up, tucking in the sides as you go. Repeat with the remaining Coconut Filling and Pancakes.

Note: To make Pandanus Juice, chop 10–20 pandanus leaves into short lengths. Place in a food processor or mini-chopper with ½ cup water (125 ml) and blend to a grassy pulp. Place the pulp in a fine sieve or a muslin bag and squeeze for deep green juice.

Gula Melaka Sago with Palm Sugar

This elegant pudding makes a perfect party dessert—it can be made ahead and is easy to prepare in multiple portions as needed.

Serves 4–5 Cooking time: 15 mins
Preparation time: 10 mins plus 1 hour standing time

150 g (1 cup) dried sago pearls, rinsed and soaked in water for 15 minutes
12 cups (3 litres) water
200 g (1 cup) shaved palm sugar or dark brown sugar
⅜ cup (100 ml) water
1 cup (250 ml) thick coconut milk
¼ teaspoon salt

1 Bring the water to a boil in a large pot. Drain the sago and add to the pot. Return to a boil and cook for 8–9 minutes or until the pearls are almost fully translucent, with just the barest white flecks in the centre of the pearls (they will continue to cook after you turn off the heat—boiling them until fully translucent makes them mushy).

2 Pour the contents of the pot through a large fine-meshed sieve and shake to drain off the excess water. Working quickly, spoon the pearls into 4 or 5 individual moulds, cups or ramekins, pressing lightly to pack them in. Let cool, then chill in the fridge for 45 minutes or until fully set.

3 Make a palm sugar syrup by combining the shaved palm sugar with the water in a small saucepan and cook over medium heat until smooth. Strain into a serving jug. In another saucepan, bring the coconut milk to a boil with the salt. Simmer for 1 minute, then pour into another serving jug and let cool.

4 To serve, turn the sago puddings onto serving bowls and top with the sauces.

Sweet Tofu and Ginkgo Dessert Soup

A traditional Chinese recipe, this dessert soup, or *tong sui*, makes an excellent, hot-weather dessert when served chilled. It is said to have cooling properties.

Serves 3–4   Cooking time: 1¼ hours
Preparation time: 5 mins

50 g (¼ cup) dried pearl barley
6 cups (1.5 litres) water
3–4 sticks twisted dried tofu skin, about 35 g (1 oz)
90 g (¼ cup) rock sugar, broken up
100 g (1 cup) canned or boiled ginkgo nuts
2 egg whites (optional)

1 Combine the barley and water in a saucepan and bring to a boil. Partially cover, reduce the heat and simmer gently for 50 minutes, or until the barley is tender and the liquid has reduced by about half.

2 Meanwhile, rinse the twisted dried tofu skins with warm water to remove any traces of oil. Tear them into large pieces.

3 Add the remaining water, rock sugar, ginkgo nuts and tofu skin to the pot and simmer, uncovered, for 10 minutes more.

4 If desired, beat the egg whites until well mixed, then slowly drizzle them into the pot in a thin stream, stirring as you pour so the whites form thin strands. Serve hot or cold.

Note: You can adjust the thickness of the dessert by increasing or reducing the amount of barley.

Cheng Thng Sweet Clear Dessert Soup

Every Chinese family has a different recipe for this classic sweet dessert soup,
which combines fruits, nuts, seeds and white fungus.

Serves 4   Cooking time: 20 mins
Preparation time: 15 mins

20 canned or boiled lotus seeds
20 canned or boiled ginkgo nuts
1 small head dried white fungus
2 dried persimmons
12 whole dried longans
4 cups (1 litre) water
2 pandanus leaves, tied into a knot
150 g (½ cup) rock sugar
1 tablespoon sugar

1 Drain the lotus seeds and ginkgo nuts and rinse under cold water. Soak the white fungus in cold water for 15 minutes or until swollen.

2 Rinse the dried persimmons and slice into 12-mm (½-in) strips, removing the hard tip. Remove the longan shells and stones and rinse the longan meats.

3 Bring the water to a boil in a large pot and add the knotted pandanus leaves, rock sugar, sugar, longan meats and dried persimmon. Simmer gently for 10 minutes.

4 Add the lotus seeds, ginkgo nuts and white fungus and simmer for another 5 minutes. Remove the pandanus leaves. Serve hot, or let cool completely and serve over crushed ice.

Wheat Pudding with Coconut Cream

This hearty and comforting porridge of wheat kernels and coconut milk is best served warm on a cool day. It does not reheat well so plan to plan halve the recipe if you're cooking for just yourself and another. Terry has a hypothesis that this has Indian origins, as "terigu" seems to be a corruption of "Telegu," where this wheat is grown.

Serves 4–5 Cooking time: 2¼ hours
Preparation time: 15 mins

300 g (1½ cups) dried white wheat kernels
2 pandanus leaves, knotted
12 cups (3 litres) water
1 cup (250 ml) thin coconut milk

Palm Sugar Syrup
200 g (1 cup) shaved palm sugar or dark brown sugar, chopped
4 tablespoons fine granulated sugar
⅔ cup (165 ml) water
½ teaspoon salt

Coconut Cream Topping
½ cup (100 ml) thick coconut milk
¼ teaspoon salt

1 Rinse the wheat and soak in cold water for 15 minutes. Drain the wheat well and combine with the pandanus leaves and water in a large pot. Bring to a boil, then reduce the heat to medium-low and simmer, partially covered, stirring occasionally, for 2 hours or until the grains have absorbed most of the water and are soft, but still have a chewy texture to them. Add more or less water for thicker or thinner texture, as desired.

2 While the wheat cooks, combine the Palm Sugar Syrup ingredients in a saucepan and cook over low heat, stirring constantly, until the sugars dissolve.

3 When the wheat is done, add the Palm Sugar Syrup to it and cook for 5 minutes, then add the coconut milk. Cook, stirring, until the mixture is just about to boil, then switch off the heat.

4 To make the Coconut Cream Topping, bring the coconut milk to a boil with the salt in a small pot over medium heat. Simmer for 1 minute, then pour into a bowl and cool. Serve the pudding with the Coconut Cream Topping on the side for guests to add by themselves.

Pandanus Chiffon Cake

Asian pandanus leaves and coconut milk infuse the American chiffon cake with a happy marriage of flavours. A time-honoured Singaporean party staple, this is often purchased nowadays but is vastly better homemade.

Serves 8–10   Cooking time: 1 hour
Preparation time: 20 mins

20–25 pandanus leaves
⅓ cup (80 ml) thick coconut milk
8 egg yolks
½ cup (125 ml) oil
250 g (1⅓ cups) cake flour
300 g (1½ cups) sugar
1½ teaspoons baking powder
⅓ teaspoon salt
8 egg whites
1 teaspoon cream of tartar

1 Preheat the oven to 160°C (325°F). Have ready a dry, ungreased 23-cm (9-in) deep round cake pan.

2 Snip the pandanus leaves into short lengths with scissors, then blend in a food processor for a few minutes until reduced to a grassy pulp. Transfer the pulp to a muslin bag or fine sieve and squeeze to obtain juice. Measure out ½ cup (125 ml) of juice (if not enough, make up difference with water) into a bowl, add the coconut milk, egg yolks and oil and whisk until smooth. Set aside.

3 Sift the cake flour into a large bowl. Add all but 3 tablespoons of the sugar, baking powder and salt. Whisk well to blend, add the egg yolk mixture and whisk until smooth.

4 In a clean bowl, beat the egg whites with the cream of tartar at high speed until soft peaks form. Gradually beat in the remaining 3 tablespoons of sugar, beating just until stiff peaks start to form. Fold the egg whites into the batter in three additions, folding just until incorporated (a few thin white streaks are okay). Pour the batter into the prepared pan, level the surface with a spatula and bake for 55–60 minutes. Cake is done when an inserted thin skewer comes out clean.

5 Invert the cake onto a rack and leave to cool upside down in the pan. Cut around the edge and base with a thin-bladed knife to release the cake from pan. Slice to serve.

Index

Acknowledgements

I had the good fortune of growing up in an extended family, with any numbers of surrogate mothers, unexplained aunts and uncles and cousins, and neighbours who enriched my life with a multitude of culinary gems. To them I dedicate this book; may it be embraced by future generations of Singaporeans with the same passion.

TERRY TAN

This book is for my grandmother, whose *kueh bangket* are without equal, and my mother, whose *kueh lapis* is without peer. To God be the glory.

CHRISTOPHER TAN

"Books to Span the East and West"

Tuttle Publishing was founded in 1832 in the small New England town of Rutland, Vermont [USA]. Our core values remain as strong today as they were then—to publish best-in-class books which bring people together one page at a time. In 1948, we established a publishing office in Japan—and Tuttle is now a leader in publishing English-language books about the arts, languages and cultures of Asia. The world has become a much smaller place today and Asia's economic and cultural influence has grown. Yet the need for meaningful dialogue and information about this diverse region has never been greater. Over the past seven decades, Tuttle has published thousands of books on subjects ranging from martial arts and paper crafts to language learning and literature—and our talented authors, illustrators, designers and photographers have won many prestigious awards. We welcome you to explore the wealth of information available on Asia at **www.tuttlepublishing.com**.

Published by Tuttle Publishing, an imprint of Periplus Editions (HK) Ltd.

Copyright ©2021 Periplus Editions (HK) Ltd (previously published as *SHIOK!*)

ISBN: 978-0-8048-5450-4
(1st edition ISBN 978-0-8048-4083-5
2nd edition ISBN 978-0-8048-4483-3)

24 23 22 21   6 5 4 3 2 1
Printed in Singapore   2107TP

Distributed by

North America, Latin America & Europe
Tuttle Publishing
364 Innovation Drive North Clarendon,
VT 05759-9436 U.S.A.
Tel: 1 (802) 773-8930; Fax: 1 (802) 773-6993
info@tuttlepublishing.com
www.tuttlepublishing.com

Japan
Tuttle Publishing Yaekari Building 3rd Floor
5-4-12 Osaki Shinagawa-ku Tokyo 141-0032
Tel: (81) 3 5437-0171; Fax: (81) 3 5437-0755
sales@tuttle.co.jp; www.tuttle.co.jp

Asia Pacific
Berkeley Books Pte. Ltd.
3 Kallang Sector #04-01
Singapore 349278
Tel: (65) 6741 2178; Fax: (65) 6741 2179
inquiries@periplus.com.sg
www.tuttlepublishing.com